Praise for Leah
Faith After Ferguson

MW01067920

"I deeply appreciate the fresh, engaging ways in which Leah Gunning Francis calls us to regain a taste for racial justice and consider how to move from what is to what ought to be. She's right: God has quite a bit to say about justice, and when we work towards forming Beloved Community it is the God who the Bible says, 'is love' who will lead us."

—The Most Rev. Michael B. Curry, Presiding Bishop of The Episcopal Church, and author of *Love is the Way: Holding on to Hope in Troubling Times*

"Leah Gunning Francis has written that rare book that is at once prophetic, pastoral, and powerful. In *Faith After Ferguson*, she holds a mirror to the face of America and shows us not just who we are, but who we ought to be. Every person who aspires to be fully human and whole, needs to read this book."

—Philip Gulley, Quaker pastor and author of *If the Church Were Christian: Rediscovering the Values of Jesus*

"With passion and scholarship, Leah Gunning Francis provides an unsparing truth about police violence and racial injustice in America. She pushes the faith community towards truth-telling and a commitment to racial justice and healing by sharing powerful, transformational stories of faith leaders and activists who are working for systemic change."

—Rev. Dr. Tracy S. Malone, Resident Bishop, Ohio East Episcopal Area, United Methodist Church

"More than recounting what has happened in Ferguson, Missouri since Michael Brown was shot and killed by a white police officer, this book reminds us there is a steadily growing list of names and cities across America where unarmed black people continue to face a similar fate. Francis quotes Rabbi Abraham Joshua Heschel who said, 'words create worlds.' The words in this book create a world of understanding about one of the most urgent issues in our country."

— Marvin A. McMickle, PhD, President (retired) Colgate Rochester Crozer Divinity School

"*Faith After Ferguson* is the powerful record of a troubled ground spring bubbling to the surface. With masterful storytelling and an ability to keep recent history alive, Leah Gunning Francis weaves facts and timelines with poignant narratives of real people doing the hard work of troubling the waters of justice. She refuses to allow us to look away from the history we are making right now, and by doing so, she insists that we do better. This important work should be taken as the warning it is—otherwise, the generations that come after us will point to it and say, 'Look. You knew. The prophets told you.' Leah Gunning Francis is that prophetic voice, and this book is a cry in the desert for a justice that is too long in coming."

— Kerry Connelly, author, *Good White Racist?: Confronting Your Role in Racial Injustice*

"In this powerful book, Dr. Leah Gunning Francis impels us to consider how far we have made odyssey towards achieving racial justice since the Ferguson uprisings of 2014. She centers the voices and experiences of the courageous activists and clergy who served on the front lines, compelling us to move beyond a mere awakening to faithful action as part of the ongoing liberation struggle for Black lives in America. This proves an essential text for all who seek in earnest to help bend the moral arc of the universe towards justice, and for it, I am exceedingly grateful. Dare to read only if you seek to transform and be transformed."

—Michael W. Waters, pastor, professor, activist, and award-winning author

FAITH
AFTER
FERGUSON

RESILIENT
LEADERSHIP
IN PURSUIT
OF RACIAL JUSTICE

LEAH GUNNING FRANCIS

chalice
press

Saint Louis, Missouri

Cover art and design: Bidemi (Bd) Oladele

Interior design: Connie Wang

ChalicePress.com

Paperback: 9780827211445

EPUB: 9780827211452

EPDF: 9780827211469

Printed in the United States of America

To Evan, Desmond, Shayla and Rodney

Stay the course.

The best is yet to come.

Contents

Acknowledgments

I wish this book did not need to be written. I wish its impetus of white supremacy, systemic racism, and police violence against Black people did not exist. But it does. I wish all churches followed in the way of Christ and were actively resisting and dismantling racial injustice. But they do not. I wish that Black children were growing up in a society that recognized and valued their humanity in the same way as their white peers. But they are not.

It is through this split lens of the *ought* and the *is* that I share stories of individuals and faith communities that are pushing back against the forces of racism to help create a more just and equitable world.

My first acknowledgment is a prayer for all of the families and loved ones of those who have been killed and for survivors who live with the scars of emotional trauma. The stories we tell and the names behind hashtags are those of actual people who once lived, moved, and had their being in families, neighborhoods, schools, and communities all around this country. And they should all be alive today. Ferguson should still be a little-known suburb of St. Louis. But it is not. My prayer is for God's peace of mind, body, and spirit for families and survivors, a peace that transcends understanding and enables them to keep on keeping on in the face of unimaginable pain and suffering. My hope is for this book to shine a small light on some of the ways that people are working to end police violence and racial injustice and that their example will entice and encourage others to join in.

This project would not have been possible without the first one, *Ferguson and Faith: Sparking Leadership and Awakening Community*. Leaders from Chalice Press and the Forum for Theological Exploration (FTE) got together and decided that we needed a book about clergy involvement in the Ferguson uprising and invited me to write it. The visioning and support of Brad Lyons and staff at Chalice Press and of Stephen Lewis, Dori Baker, and Matthew Williams at the Forum for Theological Exploration helped make that book idea a reality. I remain deeply grateful for the support and confidence that Chalice Press extended to me for this current project. Thank you, Brad, for your unwavering encouragement, and Deborah Arca, for the kind ways that you helped me think about the potential impact of this work. To my editor extraordinaire, Ulrike Guthrie: I am forever grateful for your wit, wisdom, and the skillful way that you helped me bring the manuscript to life. To our graphic designer, Connie Wang, and cover art designer Bidemi (Bd) Oladele, thank you so much for depicting this challenging story in such a beautiful way.

For the dozens of people who were willing to share their personal stories or those of their faith communities with me, I give thanks. It is not easy to permit yourself to become vulnerable and talk from a place that is intrinsic to the soul of your being. I loved spending time with each of you and listening to the different ways that you give voice to your experiences. Your stories made me laugh and cry, gasp, and grin. It was my deep honor and joy to hold space as you shared from your heart. Thank you!

When I wrote *Ferguson and Faith*, I lived in St. Louis and was a proud faculty member at Eden Seminary. The encouragement and support I received from the Eden community was exemplary. Now I serve as the dean at Christian Theological Seminary in Indianapolis. Writing and "deaning" don't exactly mix well. However, the support of our president, Dr. David Mellott, and faculty has helped my writing process significantly. I am also heartened that so many of our students are wrestling with issues related to racial injustice and their implications for faith communities. Many are already engaged in praxis-oriented justice efforts as students, and I look forward seeing the work that is yet to come.

Lastly, my heart is filled with gratitude for my family and friends. I am blessed beyond measure to have such a wonderful community of love and support. My parents, Dan and Martha Gunning, laid the foundation of love and justice upon which I stand proudly today. My last living grandparent, Louise Drake, continues to be a source of strength and wisdom for this leg of my journey. My younger siblings, Carla and Drake, are always at the ready to dole out laughs at their sister's expense. My beloved children are more wonderful than anything I could have ever imagined. And for the joy of my loving in-laws, extended family and many friends that are much more like family than acquaintances, I am grateful for the heart ties that bind us together.

When I was in my early thirties, I wasn't sure if I would ever find a life partner. Then one day, out of the blue, my dear friend Greg Ellison said to me, "Leah, I have someone I want you to meet." And the rest is history. Rev. Rodney Francis and I have been married for fifteen fantastic years. Thank you, Rodney, for all of the love, support, and laughter you give each day. It would not have been possible for me to adequately care for Desmond and Evan, work full-time, *and* complete this project without all of your efforts. Thanks be to God for the wonderful gift of you.

Introduction

"Mommy, has Michael Brown gotten any justice yet?"

I froze. What was prompting our young son to ask this question?

Eight months had passed since a Ferguson police officer had killed Michael Brown. Had our son had a dream about Michael or about the ensuing Ferguson uprising? How should I respond?

I decided to tell him truth, gently.

"No, son. Michael Brown hasn't received the justice we were hoping for. But we're going to keep working at it."

I didn't burden him with the whole truth. I didn't tell him that many people hoped the police officer who killed Michael would be held fully accountable, how they hoped that police departments around the country would immediately review their policies and protocols and enforce a de-escalation practice as a first line of defense. I couldn't tell him of our hopes being dashed that we would not see this type of killing again—and again and again.

A police officer shot Ezell Ford in the back after being stopped while walking down a Los Angeles street.

Kajieme Powell was shot twelve times on a St. Louis sidewalk.

Laquan McDonald's seventeen-year-old body lay smoking on a Chicago street, riddled with six bullets.

Within three seconds of arriving on the scene, police officers near Cleveland shot and killed twelve-year-old Tamir Rice who had been playing alone on a playground with a toy gun.

A police officer shot Walter Scott in the back in Charleston, South Carolina, and planted a taser next to his lifeless body.

Near Atlanta, a police officer shot and killed a completely naked Anthony Hill, a US Air Force veteran.

Freddie Gray died of spinal cord injuries police inflicted on him while in police custody in Baltimore.

Police stopped and arrested Sandra Bland for an alleged traffic violation. She died mysteriously in a jail cell in the tiny town of Waller County, Texas.

Police stopped Philando Castile, a Montessori school employee who knew every child's name, for an unknown reason near St. Paul, Minnesota, and shot him six times in his car with his girlfriend and daughter only inches away.

Instead of helping him, police shot and killed Terence Crutcher beside his broken-down car in Tulsa, Oklahoma.

None of these incidents happened in the same city, town, or state. None of them happened at the same exact time of day. The victims varied in age and circumstance. The one thing they all had in common was the color of their skin. They were all African American. This is a hard truth to tell a child—and even an adult—but it is a truth that adults must confront if we are going to create a society that makes possible liberty and justice for *all*.

Just when we could not imagine how police contact with Black people could get any worse, in 2020 the world witnessed a Minneapolis police officer kneel on the neck of George Floyd, a Black man accused of passing a counterfeit $20 bill, for 8 minutes and 46 seconds as Floyd begged him to stop. *"Please man...I can't breathe,"* Floyd muttered as he gasped for air. Bystanders begged the officer to stop. "He is a human being!" shouted one of the onlookers. For 8 minutes and 46 seconds the pleas fell on deaf and uncaring ears until Floyd took his last breath and lay unconscious on the asphalt at 38th and Chicago Avenue.

This public execution came on the heels of that of Breonna Taylor, a twenty-six-year-old ER technician in Louisville, Kentucky, whom police fatally shot in the middle of the night after they burst into her home allegedly looking for drugs, and the murder of Ahmaud Arbery, a twenty-five-year-old who was jogging in the middle of the day while Black, whom neighborhood vigilantes deemed "suspect" and shot to death in Brunswick, Georgia. All of this happened in the middle of a global pandemic known as COVID-19.

In the aftermath of Brown's killing by a Ferguson police officer, a movement of resistance and resilience emerged, the likes of which had not been seen since the Civil Rights Movement. Young people took to the streets of the St. Louis region and were soon joined by people of all ages, colors, and abilities. News media outlets from around the world stationed themselves in the area for months. Social media platforms like Twitter (whose CEO and co-founder happens to be from St. Louis) became a go-to source for the most current and accurate information.

This movement for racial justice sparked by the killing of an unarmed young Black man was broadcast around the world in unprecedented ways; however, in this era the story was not controlled solely by corporate news media outlets. The pictures, videos, and live interviews that were provided by people who were participating in the marches or vigils offered an unfiltered look into the events as they were. There were no production managers or editorial directors working to frame their narratives to fit the goals of a news company's agenda. Instead, the agenda of the street "reporters" was to tell the truth as they saw it and give context and voice to what was happening.

It was the first time in history that the public was not largely dependent on news media outlets to learn about such a massive event.

In 1994, renowned Nigerian author and poet Chinua Achebe in an interview with the *Paris Review* talked about his journey to becoming a writer, storyteller, and social critic. He emphasized the importance of telling our own stories and said, "There is that great proverb: until the lions have their own historians, the history of the hunt will always glorify the hunter."

The victims of the hunt now have their own historians—bloggers, vloggers, Twitter users, and so on. The narratives about what happened that fateful day on Canfield Drive and the movement for racial justice that was born again in Ferguson were not confined to the news media and its pundits, to police reports, or to the writings of professional journalists. The stories that the people most intimately affected by the tragedy and those committed to the struggle for racial justice in this country were producing, the public deemed to be trustworthy and valid. Even after the news cameras left, protests and various acts of resistance occurred...and the truth continued to be told.

Michael Brown's mother, Lezley McSpadden, shared one particularly compelling story. In 2016, she published a book titled *Tell the Truth & Shame the Devil: The Life, Legacy and Love of My Son Michael Brown*, in which she writes candidly about her life and family, raising

"Mike Mike," and pivotal moments before and after Mike's death.[1]

In what was undoubtedly the worst day of her life, she described the scene on Canfield Drive after she'd tried for hours to get information about what happened to her son. She writes:

> Me and Brittanie slowly moved toward the bloodstained pavement where Mike Mike's body had been left under the baking sun and stood in a daze, and I began shaking my head. "Why?" I called out. The police had left him out there like he wasn't nobody's. But I needed them and the rest of the world to know that Mike Mike did belong to somebody, a whole damn family, and he was mine before he was anybody else's. A crowd of strangers gathered around, chanting, "Hands up! Don't shoot!" A hand reached through the crowd and handed me a bouquet of roses. I pulled off each rose petal and dropped it on the pavement, covering what was now sacred ground to me.[2]

McSpadden goes on to describe what happened when a local news reporter asked her what information the police had given her thus far. She responded:

> They haven't told me anything. They wouldn't even let me identify my son. The only way I knew it was my son was from people out here showing me his picture on the Internet!... "He threw his hands up! He ain't have no gun. The boy threw his hands up, and the police just shot him," I heard a woman yell from the crowd....I was begging the police for answers, but my words fell on deaf ears. The cop who killed my son had vanished into thin air. My son was gone.[3]

Michael Brown was Lezley McSpadden and Michael Brown Sr.'s son. He was loved by his parents, grandparents, siblings, aunts, uncles, and cousins. He was a human being. As his mother said, he *belonged* to them, and she details the contours of that belonging throughout

---

[1] Lezley McSpadden, *Tell the Truth & Shame the Devil: The Life, Legacy and Love of My Son Michael Brown* (New York: Regan Arts, 2016).

[2] McSpadden, *Tell the Truth*, 182.

[3] McSpadden, *Tell the Truth*, 184.

her memoir. Her account and the many other accounts by those who knew Mike Mike differ sharply from the police report and the media accounts. It's impossible to say with certainty what we would know about this tragic story if the news media outlets were our only source of information. We don't know for sure what our understanding of the situation would be if there had been no tweets, no Facebook posts, and no Periscope livestreams. However, my hunch is that the truth was generated from the on-the-ground perspectives in St. Louis from everyday people who, as Fannie Lou Hamer says, were "sick and tired of being sick and tired." That truth struck a chord with thousands around the world.

There was too much collective memory about Trayvon Martin, Oscar Grant, and Rodney King—to name a few—for these on-the-ground accounts to be dismissed easily. The young people in Ferguson took to the streets and declared "Enough!" and there was a worldwide chorus that responded "Amen!"

* * *

As I write in early 2021, seven years have passed since Ferguson became what we now know as #Ferguson. Many people have asked, "What's happened in St. Louis since the Ferguson uprising? What has changed? Did all of those protests make a difference?" While neither I nor anyone else has a comprehensive answer to these questions, I was interested in learning more about what has happened in St. Louis related to racial justice since the uprising and about what's happened in the lives of some of the people I interviewed for *Ferguson and Faith: Sparking Leadership and Awakening Community*.[4] That book is collection of narratives from more than two dozen clergy and young activists who were active participants and leaders in the movement for racial justice in Ferguson. Through their stories, we saw aspects of the movement and its events through their eyes and learned about the faith that fueled and inspired them to get involved.

In the years since then, I followed up with more than a dozen of the people I'd interviewed previously, and included a few new ones. All of them were clergy and young activists who spent a significant amount of time, energy, and resources engaging the movement for racial justice in St. Louis and beyond. I wanted to know how their involvement has impacted their lives, what they have learned, and what pathways to a

---

[4] Leah Gunning Francis, *Ferguson and Faith: Sparking Leadership and Awakening Community* (St. Louis, MO: Chalice Press, 2015).

future filled with hope look like. And I wanted to know what role faith has played in their lives. In *Ferguson and Faith*, they detailed the ways in which their faith compelled them to take action in the movement. What have they learned since then about faith-filled living in response to social injustice? What can the church and communities of faith learn from their experiences about God's ongoing call to join God's transforming work in the world?

One of the ways that people referenced the movement for racial justice was as an *awakening*. This was especially true for many people who are not considered members of a racial or ethnic minority. They hadn't realized how pervasive and systemic the problem of racial injustice is in our country. Many assumed that the election of a Black president was an indication of the country "moving beyond" racism and discrimination. Ferguson shattered that myth for many and revealed in our collective body a fissure in urgent need of attention. The hashtag #staywoke began to circulate among social media platforms encouraging people to not go back to business as usual, but to use their awakening moment as a catalyst to work towards eradicating racial injustice.

Over the past few years I have thought a lot about the idea of *awakening* and the need to #staywoke. While no two awakenings look exactly alike, I've learned that there are some particular things we should do to remain awake. After many conversations, forums, workshops, and engagements, I have concluded that once we perceive ourselves to have been *awakened, staying awake cannot merely be a cognitive exercise.* In other words, if we are to wake up and recognize all of the ways that racial injustice exists in our everyday lives—personally and systemically—and work to end this injustice, we must employ all of our senses to do so. It cannot merely be an intellectual exercise where one says, "Oh, I believe that racism exists." Instead, we must bring all of our senses to bear—sight, hearing, taste, touch, and smell—in order to help us discern and understand where and how racism exists and what we can do to eradicate it.

Throughout the book, I invite you to engage in sensory work as a way to delve deeper into the scope of racial injustice in our world. To remain awake to the presence of racial injustice and the ways we can eradicate it, we must awaken and engage all of our senses in this transformative work. The wisdom that emerges out of the following stories challenges us all to awaken all of our senses, and it equips us to join God's transformative work of racial justice.

Timeline of Selected Events Since the Ferguson Uprising

2014

August 19: Kajieme Powell, 25, shot and killed by a St. Louis, MO police officer

October 8: VonDerrit Myers, 18, shot and killed by a St. Louis, MO police officer working as a security guard

October 20: Laquan McDonald, 17, shot 16 times by a Chicago, IL police officer

November 22: Tamir Rice, 12, shot and killed by a Cleveland, OH area police officer on a playground

2015

April 4: Walter Scott, 50, shot in the back and killed by a Charleston, SC police officer

April 19: Freddie Gray, 25, died of spinal cord injuries after being in Baltimore, MD police custody

June 17: Mother Emanuel Church massacre where 9 people were killed in Charleston, SC

July 13: Sandra Bland, 28, died in Waller County, TX jail after a police traffic stop

2016

April 1: Dakota Access Pipeline protests began at the Standing Rock Reservation

June 12: Pulse Nightclub Massacre in Orlando, FL where 49 people were killed

July 5: Alton Sterling, 37, shot and killed by two Baton Rouge, LA Police officers

July 6: Philando Castile, 32, shot and killed by a Minneapolis, MN area officer during a traffic stop

July 7: Five police officers killed in Dallas, TX by an Army Reserve Afghanistan war Veteran

Sept. 1: 49ers quarterback Colin Kaepernick first kneeled during the playing of the National Anthem

Sept. 16: Terence Crutcher, 40, shot and killed by Tulsa, OK police officer beside his disabled car

Nov. 8: Donald Trump, elected president of the United States

2017

Jan. 21: Women's March in Washington, DC and across the country to protest Donald Trump's election

June 29: Aaron Bailey, 45, shot and killed by two Indianapolis, IN police officers

Aug. 11–12: Unite the Right protests in Charlottesville, VA against Confederate statue removals

Sept. 15: Officer Jason Stockley acquitted of murdering Anthony L. Smith in St. Louis, MO in 2011

Oct. 1: Shooting at concert goers outside the Mandalay Bay Hotel in Las Vegas, NV left at least 58 dead

Oct: #METOO Sexual assault and awareness campaign goes viral

Nov 5: Shooting at First Baptist Church in Sutherland Springs, TX left 26 dead

2018

Feb. 14: 17 students and adults shot and killed at Marjory S. Douglas HS in Parkland, FL

June: 700 protests across the country against migrant family separations

Sept. 6: Botham Jean, 26, shot to death in his own apartment by a Dallas, TX police officer

Oct 27: Tree of Life Synagogue shooting left 11 people dead in Pittsburgh, PA

2019

Jan. 14–22: Los Angeles, CA teachers strike as part of the Red for Ed movement

Aug. 3: A mass shooting at a Walmart in El Paso, TX left 23 people dead

Aug. 25: Elijah McClain, 23, stopped while walking down the street by Aurora, CO police and died after being injected with ketamine

Oct. 4: Joshua Brown, 28, a key witness in the case against the police officer who killed Botham Jean, was shot and killed two days after the trial ended

2020

Jan. 26: Basketball legend Kobe Bryant, daughter Gianna, and 6 others killed in a helicopter crash in Calabasas, CA

Feb. 23: Ahmaud Arbery, 25, shot and killed by two white men while jogging in Brunswick, GA

March: Schools and businesses began to close due to the emergence of COVID-19

March 13: Breonna Taylor, 26, shot and killed by plainclothes officers who burst into her home in the middle of the night in Louisville, KY

May 6: Dreasjon Reed, 21, shot and killed by an Indianapolis, IN police officer

May 25: George Floyd, 46, died on a Minneapolis, MN street after a police officer pinned him under his knee

June 12: Rayshard Brooks, 27, shot and killed by an Atlanta, GA police officer

Nov. 7: Joe Biden and Kamala Harris elected as president and vice president

Dec. 25: Christmas Day bombing in downtown Nashville, TN displaced more than 400 residents and affected at least 45 businesses

2021

Jan. 6: Insurrection at the US Capitol in an attempt to stop the certification of election results

Memorial to Michael Brown, Jr.
Canfield Apartments, Ferguson, Missouri *(Photos by Leah Gunning Francis)*

CHAPTER 1

....

This *is* Us

"Let me be very clear. The scenes of chaos at the Capitol do not reflect a true America, do not represent who we are!" said President-elect Joe Biden as he stood resolutely to condemn the US Capitol invasion on January 6, 2021. Thousands of people, at the behest of President Trump, had made their way to Washington, DC, to object forcefully to the certification of the election of President-elect Joe Biden and the first woman Vice President-elect, Kamala Harris.

Since the election was called for Biden and Harris on November 7, the President had ramped up his "Stop the Steal" movement that claimed him to be the victim of an allegedly rigged election. In citing mostly Black and Latinx jurisdictions in Atlanta, Detroit, and Philadelphia (to name a few) as the scenes of the crimes, he played into the racist stereotype that "those people" could not be trusted.[5]

On the morning of November 7, President Trump tweeted an alert that his lawyers would hold a press conference at Four Seasons in Philadelphia at 11:00 a.m.; however, the posh downtown hotel had no press conference on its schedule. The president soon deleted that tweet and clarified the location of the press conference that officially launched the "Stop the Steal" movement: The Four Seasons Total Landscaping parking lot in northeast Philly, next door to an "adult" bookstore and across from the street from the Delaware Valley Cremation Center. Rudy Giuliani, former NYC mayor turned Trump attorney, claimed massive voter fraud. Yet after snaking their case

---

[5] Kristine Phillips, "'Damaging to Our Democracy': Trump Election Lawsuits Targeted Areas with Large Black, Latino Populations," USA Today (Gannett Satellite Information Network, December 1, 2020), https://www.usatoday.com/story/news/politics/2020/12/01/trump-voter-fraud-claims-target-counties-more-black-latino-votes/6391908002.

through multiple courts, no fraud was to be found anywhere. However, "alternative facts" were one of the hallmarks of this administration, so its cronies were not deterred by the legal rulings.

President Trump and his surrogates continued to claim voter fraud and strongly encouraged his supporters to meet in DC on January 6. During his speech before the massive crowd, he refused to concede and encouraged them to walk to the Capitol to "try and give our Republicans, the weak ones, because the strong ones don't need any of our help, we're going to try and give them the kind of pride and boldness that they need to take back our country.[6]" When the crowd arrived at the Capitol sans the president, they were met by the Capitol police, who were quickly overwhelmed by the size and aggressiveness of the crowd. Surprisingly, there were no National Guard members staggered on the Capitol steps like they had been on the Lincoln Memorial steps during a peaceful protest of the death of George Floyd.[7] As a result, Capitol police were pushed, shoved, beaten, and quickly overrun by the mob rushing up the Capitol stairs. However, none of these officers felt sufficiently threatened or feared sufficiently for their lives to fire their weapons. As the insurgents busted out windows and forced their way into the Capitol, Vice President Pence was whisked away to an undisclosed location. Congress members took cover as best they could as rioters invaded and vandalized the building and accomplished a feat that the Confederate Army could not: marching the Confederate flag through the US Capitol. Five people died that day and scores more were physically and psychologically injured. However, some of the insurrectionists were able to take selfies with Capitol police before they moseyed out of the building like tourists.

My response to President-elect Biden's defiant statement about this not being representative of who we are is adamant: This *is* who we are. And until we resolve to open our eyes and see the truth that is staring back at us, we will continue to fall prey to the belief that we are "better than this." History does not support that claim. The scores of unarmed Black people that police have killed since Ferguson doesn't

---

[6] Brian Naylor, "Read Trump's Jan. 6 Speech, A Key Part of Impeachment Trial." NPR (Feb. 10, 2021). https://www.npr.org/2021/02/10/966396848/read-trumps-jan-6-speech-a-key-part-of-impeachment-trial. Accessed February 12, 2021.

[7] Tyler Clifford, "Philadelphia Mayor Blasts Double Standard in Policing of Black and White Protestors." CNBC Politics (NBC Universal, January 7, 2021). https://www.cnbc.com/2021/01/07/philadelphia-mayor-blasts-double-standard-in-policing-black-and-white-protesters.html Accessed January 7, 2021.

give that claim a leg to stand on. The pervasiveness of poverty, and its corresponding effects, in one of the wealthiest countries in the world would prevent that case from holding up in a court of law. And these are just a few of the rationales that contest that myth.

For me, the truth is not that we *are* "better than this," but that we *can and should be* "better than this." In tragic irony, the Capitol invasion happened on Epiphany, the day that the Christian church celebrates the Magi's visit to the newborn Jesus. The word epiphany in Greek can be translated as a manifestation, an appearance, or *to come suddenly into view*. A person says, "I had an epiphany" to describe an "aha" moment that brought clarity and insight to a situation.

> *After Jesus was born in Bethlehem in Judea, during the time of King Herod, Magi from the east came to Jerusalem and asked "Where is the one who has been born king of the Jews? We saw his star in the east and have come to worship."*[8]

As the Magi made their way to Jesus, King Herod summoned them under the false pretense that he too wanted to go and worship Jesus. He insisted that as soon as they found him, they come back and tell him where Jesus was located. The Magi followed the eastern star to find Jesus.

> *On coming to the house, they saw the child with his mother Mary, and they bowed down and worshiped him. Then they opened their treasures and presented him with gifts of gold and incense and of myrrh. And having been warned in a dream not to go back to Herod, they returned to their country by another route.*[9]

Thankfully, the Magi heeded the warning and did not go back to Herod. I have long been nudged by this text to remember that once you get some good and reliable intel, act on it—even if it means going in a different direction than planned.

What if we took the intel, or the truth, that was shown to us through the Capitol invasion and decided to return to our notion of being a country by another route? What if we let go of the myth that we are "better than this," the idols of white supremacy and Christian

---

[8] Matthew 2:1–2, New International Version.
[9] Matthew 2:11–12, New International Version.

nationalism, the lie of American exceptionalism and the bootstraps ideology, and instead charted a new course to become truly "better than this?" I imagine it wasn't easy for the Magi to find a new route home. They probably had to ask around to find Jesus' house. I can only imagine how hard it was to figure out how to sneak out of town without running into King Herod or his posse. But they knew they couldn't go back the same way. Neither should we. If we are determined to follow a pathway toward a future filled with hope and flourishing for all, we cannot get there by traveling the well-worn road of racism. Instead, we must chart a new course that challenges the status quo, heeds the voices of those who have been marginalized and dehumanized, yet realize that this will become the path of most resistance. Empire *will* strike back. However, the stories throughout this book remind us that ordinary people have banded together to do extraordinary things to make a difference. You can too.

We Have Become an Organizing City

The Ferguson uprising in 2014 sparked a renewed wave of sustained movements for racial justice. Various forms of protest occurred in the months and years following the killing of Michael Brown throughout the St. Louis region. One of the questions I routinely receive is "What has changed in St. Louis?" While there are myriad ways to answer this question, the organization and mobilization efforts are notable.

Brittany Ferrell is an activist, mom, nurse, and scholar who was an early and long-standing fixture on the frontlines in Ferguson. Since the Ferguson uprising, Brittany has earned a Master in Public Health from Washington University and is currently a PhD student in their Nursing Science program. Her resilience is reflected in her ongoing justice work that includes the professional integration of health and wellness for Black people. She says:

> One thing that has changed in St. Louis is that we have become an organizing city. We now have organizations like Action St. Louis, The Bail Project, and Arch City Defenders who are doing great organizing work. Action St. Louis was campaigning to get Bob McCulloch out of office and was very successful in doing that with the #ByeBob campaign— with Bob McCulloch being the prosecutor who was in office when Michael Brown was murdered and who failed to find

Darren Wilson guilty for killing Michael Brown. It's been years of pushing back against the system, of organizing, of strategizing on how we can get even a small victory out of such a tragic, tragic story.

Getting Bob McCulloch out of office was a big win not just for Michael Brown and Ferguson and St. Louis but for people around the country to watch how a movement has made strong, tenacious organizers who have found something in themselves that has kept them in doing this work for so many years—even when everyone has left, when all of the cameras have left, when all of the writers are no longer doing stories on Ferguson or St. Louis. People are still doing that work and so that was a huge, huge, huge win.

The resources are now coming into young, Black-led organizations. Kayla Reed is leading Action St. Louis where most of the organizers are in their twenties. The Bail Project is young Black folks, and Arch City Defenders are attorneys who are levering their assets and doing work around closing the Workhouse and ending cash bail and debtor's prisons. And now we have the resources to be able to do very, very important work since then. And more people are aware of it. More people want to be a part of it. That's one thing that makes me very, very happy. I joined the Close the Workhouse campaign which is a part of Action St. Louis and Arch City Defenders. Seeing that mass incarceration and the conditions of the Workhouse are a huge public health problem and trying to leverage my access to the institution where I'm currently enrolled and the resources that I have available to me to do work around the issue. It's like being able to improve the conditions for some in this city and to know that you have a place to do it now. I think that's pretty incredible.

Almost everyone with whom I spoke pointed to Wesley Bell's election as the St. Louis County prosecutor as one of the biggest "wins" since the Ferguson uprising, as well as other state and local elections. DeMarco Davidson worked with the Bell campaign and shared his thoughts about Bell and what surprised him most about the election:

Wesley Bell is an African American attorney who was running for the St. Louis County prosecutor against Bob McCulloch, the prosecuting attorney who failed to bring charges against Darren Wilson, the police officer who killed Michael Brown, Jr. Wesley grew up in St. Louis County and was very active in the community. He was a lawyer, and he was elected to become a Ferguson City Council member in 2015. He'd always promoted progressive laws especially when it came to helping people since his time as a public defender even before Ferguson happened. Many people knew him and trusted him. They had a great amount of trust in his ability to help fix what is broken in the system. There were a lot of different kinds of people that supported him. A huge amount of pastors were really supportive of Wesley. On the Sunday before the election, we went to ten different churches, and Wesley was allowed a chance to speak. This so helpful because not everyone opened their doors for people to talk about things involving Ferguson back in 2014. So to see that change happen was great. I really believe they understood that they had to be on the right side of history this time. And the young people who were fourteen at the time are now eighteen, and they were adamant about voting.

I was extremely surprised by two different things. First, there were police officers that were excited about the prospect of a new prosecuting attorney. I didn't believe it until I saw a police chief from one of the municipalities come and actually donate money toward Wesley. There were police officers that believed that Bob McCulloch made their job harder and created a rift in the fabric of the community. Trust was not there. I was also surprised to see how enthusiastic so many white people were about his candidacy. There were many who recognized how racist the justice system was and interpreted Bob McCulloch's actions [of] not pressing any charges against the officer who killed Michael Brown, Jr. [as racist.] It was a perfect storm of events. There were young and old, Black and white who worked together to get him elected. The activist groups like Action St. Louis and Color of Change and Missouri Faith Voices helped lead too. All of this made #ByeBob possible.

Rev. Dr. Karen Anderson was the pastor of Ward Chapel AME Church in Florissant during the Ferguson uprising. In 2019, Bishop Clement Fugh appointed her to serve as the senior pastor of First AME Church in Las Vegas, Nevada. Rev. Anderson is the first woman to hold this position at First AME. She highlights the organizing efforts that led to Bell's success and beyond:

Wesley Bell speaking at protest in downtown St. Louis. *(Photo courtesy of DeMarco Davidson)*

When Wesley Bell was elected, I think it showed the power of organizing and having a very succinct message, and it was organization. People got out and worked. They worked hard to shift the balance of power. They worked hard to ensure that he would get that seat. In our AME denomination, in my district, the bishop this year is talking the year of Pentecost. It's that idea of being on one accord. For some reason, what our new prosecuting attorney said resonated with a lot of people. And it brought people in one accord to say it's time for something different. There was a sense of his honesty and transparency.

And I think that there had been enough animus against McCulloch for the poor way he handled Michael Brown and that there were enough people who were still angry about how that happened and that they understood that a change needed to happen. I think there are times when people get so comfortable in their place of power that their outward attitude is that I'm here and there's nothing you can do about it. And I think, every once in a while, that causes the hairs on the back of people's necks to stand up, and they make a decision that something has to change. But it was also the fact that it registered with a lot of people across race and that socioeconomic status. His team was a very diverse group of people that he had on the ground working for him. And it was huge, and it wasn't a small margin. He won by quite a bit.

In 2016, we began to really look at voter engagement and ask, "How do we help to organize the community around the issues that are coming up on the ballots during election years?" We worked really hard trying to fight against the voter ID bill that passed in Missouri. Unfortunately, we weren't successful, but we learned from it.

One of the things we learned was that you have to have multiple contacts with people. Just knocking on a door one time isn't enough; you have to follow up with a phone call and try and find out about the issues that are important to them. We're learning how to mobilize people and get people energized around the issues that are important to them in their local communities, because sometimes we're so focused on national elections that we overlook the local issues. Local issues have a greater impact on people's lives, and we have to work together to address them.

For example, we worked with Missouri Jobs for Justice, Fight for 15, Raise Up Missouri around raising the minimum wage and Clean Missouri around campaign financing. We were successful in this election at getting the minimum wage raised. People in Missouri still made $7.65 an hour which means they would make about $314 a week. Who can live on that? It's not going to be raised overnight but within the next two years, it will go up to at least $12 an hour. This is an issue that was important to a lot of people.

Rev. Dr. Dietra Wise Baker is a lead organizer with Metropolitan Congregations United and the former pastor of Liberation Christian Church. Dr. Baker and her husband welcomed their first child in 2018. She reflects on the organizing efforts that are happening around Missouri to create rural and urban coalitions:

St. Louis activists Jessica Wernli, Michelle Higgins, Kristian Blackmon, Brittini Gray, and Kayla Reed at a protest on November 3, 2015. *(Photo by Sean Loftin)*

One of the things [that] I think is going great in St. Louis is that people respond to political/racial/justice issues now. I don't think you can go to anything and there's not going to be a small crowd. White and Black people are obviously more awake and way more participatory and responsive. Some of the grassroots organizations that were very volunteer-based have grown to have multiple staff people. They've grown their infrastructure and their missions after Ferguson in ways that we didn't expect but always hoped for. We have a good, strong base of organizations [that] are stronger and have a little bit more capacity to organize into the future.

Another positive development is the MOVE Collaboration (Missouri Organizing and Voter Engagement). Dr. Manuel Pastor's work on changing demographics shows that Missouri won't become a majority people of color state when a lot of other states will. We'll still be a majority white state. The collaborative has taken this demographic information and has worked to build a Black rural collaborative for voter engagement and to work alongside...issue work. It also has the Organization for Black Struggle, and the Rural Crisis Center, which is mostly made up of farmers. It has Faith in Action, which is another faith-based organizing group like MCU, and Jobs with Justice, which brings us into a relationship with our labor folks. So you've got faith and labor, and urban and rural collaborations working together. We have a lot of work to do and [in] every campaign we work on we're constantly building our capacity, tactics, and strategy to get more and more people involved in building the civic infrastructure of our local, state, and national communities. So that's what's happening in Missouri.

Rev. Rebecca Ragland is the pastor of St. Paul's Episcopal Church, Carondolet in St. Louis and has long been active in the protest movement. During the Ferguson uprising she was the director for the Episcopal Service Corp and shares her reflections on that experience.

Several things I think have changed for good. For one, I think we have significant representation at the state level from our St. Louis State Representative Bruce Franks and in the local elections with Rasheen Aldridge. There are others who really grew out of the Ferguson uprising in terms of having clarity about their voice and vision and that to me, is the close down the Workhouse movement, tending the cash bail system, advocating for that, the level of responsiveness in this community to issues, to just get out there and endorse and show support, it seems hugely to be modeled and to have sort of begun during Ferguson.

Brittini Gray is poet, writer, activist and Eden Seminary graduate. She has provided significant leadership for the protest movements and in the development of alternative movement spaces that focus on the arts and healing. She reflects:

I think it's harder to see the evidence of movements where they are born rather than where they inspire. And so there have been small policy wins. I look at the election of Wesley Bell as a victory and getting McCulloch out of office. We're at that time period where movements become institutionalized. And so how it looks, in terms of what people are doing, where spaces exist is going to be different than how it looked when folks were all gathering outside to protest. And I look at how the Black Healers Collective has been an outgrowth of that or how more things like Black-on-Black Friday is becoming such a gathering space after Thanksgiving for people in the community to go out and actually support Black businesses in a way that you wouldn't have seen this many people at that in 2013. So it's really a catch-22 [situation] for me in terms of how you see the impact of a movement space and just being very aware that people have gone back to their everyday lives. And so, if folks are not integrating what justice looks like in their own lives, they've just become accustomed to things being the way that they are again.

So when I just look at what our current movement spaces are, you still have what people refer to as Black Lives Matters or Movement for Black Lives, even though those are specific organizations—just the movement space that honors Black people. And then you have things like Me Too being able to really take hold. I see all of that, even the rebellion against our current [Trump] administration, as being rooted in coming up in a time where public displays of protests are the norm. It gives space for people to express in public about what's wrong in society. I think all of our systems that do not seek to benefit people but prey on places where we are not as organized, places where folks do not have decision-making power over their lives, are being called out. And that's every system. I think that's policing. I think it's the healthcare system. I think it's our education system. All of these systems are now being analyzed more critically and appropriately. This is true for policing where all the accusations that come out about how the policing culture is toxic and is founded on a system that was always meant for oppression should rightfully make people's jobs harder. I think people that function as gatekeepers to the status quo have to be challenged in those spaces that they occupy.

Building political power: No middle ground

The impetus to build political power to prioritize the needs of the most vulnerable and give voice to the lived experiences of marginalized people was evident throughout the Ferguson uprising and in the years since. However, these priorities cannot survive on "middle ground"— or between two radically opposed ideologies. Clarity of purpose and priority proved essential for many St. Louis area voters and others.

Michelle Higgins is the co-chair of Action St. Louis and reflects on grassroots organizing that has contributed to the political successes:

> I think that shift has gone from the experience of protest to the experience of politics and defeating Bob McCulloch was huge. When Action St. Louis canvassed Ferguson, our lead organizer for #ByeBob was Rodney Brown and our lead communication director, Karissa Anderson, and then my co-chair, Kayla Reed, who all helped lead that campaign to say to people, "When you say to yourself don't forget about this murder, don't forget about this injustice, take that rage and produce a win. You can take your justified anger and produce something that brings transformative healing."
>
> We talk a lot about transformative change because of the Ferguson Commission, and I think that a lot of the language that we use is thanks to people like Rev. Dr. Starsky Wilson and the crew at Deaconess and how they basically show us that toxic philanthropy is not only real, but it's ripping resources out of actual grassroots organizations. The Ferguson protestors challenged the mess out of toxic philanthropists. One of my job contracts looks at and

critiques the way that charities do charity work. And the Deaconess Foundation promotes that kind of analysis because philanthropy can be capitalistic. And I think that people like the Ferguson protestors helped to change that.

Politics, philanthropy, and policing as well. In 2014, if somebody said, "We think that low level crimes in St. Louis just shouldn't be prosecuted," folks would [have been] like, "That's ridiculous!" But here we are, four plus years later, and it's just part of being progressive. I think the actions of protest have made it so that, if you live in St. Louis and someone is demanding change, even if you don't want to listen to the way that we shut down streets or the way that we yell in the middle of city council or board of [*laughs*] aldermen meetings, [*laughs*] even if you're mad when we shut down the Ways and Means Committee and all these things in City Hall or the Galleria mall multiple times— you pay attention. Language changes, and what the average citizen of St. Louis is open to hearing and discussing has begun to change. I think the big turning point, at least for me, was to see Tishaura Jones's campaign for mayor, and her bold stance on racial justice. She damned diversity. She was like, "this is just optics. We will not do the tokenizing *Hey-I-hired-some-Black-people* checkmarks and gold stars."

She insisted that was not enough. She made it clear that she was serious about a living wage, and it was a bold statement because it is not centrist. Centrism would say, "I hear that these people aren't making enough, and I hear that a living wage is costly." The Ferguson activists and the St. Louis activist community are not impressed by centrism. Look at what happened to Claire McCaskill's campaign. She went centrist which means, eventually, you just side with racists. Centrism is Donald Trump saying [there are] nice people on both sides.

There is no centrism that keeps my people alive in this era of anti-Blackness. Tishaura's boldness and honesty almost won the day. Lyda Krewson ran a centrist campaign supported by the police, claimed to pursue racial equity, and reminded us that she was in with the Ferguson Commission. Centrism won, but Tishaura's campaign came so close and it brought such a challenge to see a woman in the legacy of Shirley Chisolm run and have people of faith, activists, your average white, crunch hipster and wealthy people follow her and say, "We're not just voting for you because your name is urban. We think you're smart. We think you know what you're doing." And that was a major shift for me because it allowed the protest action to be funneled into political involvement.

Radical civic engagement has to be the counterpart to radical disruption for the sake of displaying truth. If I know that there's something under the surface of my country, like the blood crying out of all the Native nations that were massacred, I have to raise that to the surface. And that truth means that I can't go back to life as usual. The status quo is destroyed. The Ferguson uprising destroyed the status quo for what people believed about police brutality and systemic racism in St. Louis.

Brittany Ferrell reflects on her evolving perspective about the saliency of voting and the need to build political power:

I used to be very "voting doesn't change anything" and with the 2018 elections and all of the voter suppression that happened in Florida and Georgia, it has taught me the importance of if we are going to exist in a society like this, while we're changing it, we must have political power. We do not have it which means that it is our responsibility to build it. And either you're going to build it or you're not and so I began to learn that building political power for Black people is a radical act in itself. And in building political power for Black people, that does not mean that it is the fix to all of our problems, but it is simply another tool that we have to use. And just a few years ago, I never would have said that. I would have said "Who cares? It doesn't work. It's not going to change anything." But now, it's different for me. It feels different. It feels like what's going to happen is that we're going to build Black political power because that's one component of what we do need in order to change our conditions year to year.

St. Louis Circuit Attorney Kim Gardner,
Candidate for US Congressional District One Cori Bush,
and St. Louis Treasurer Tishaura Jones at a press
conference on August 6, 2020. *(Photo by Philip Deitch)*

I've started working with the Black Futures Lab where I'm doing more political work around policy and advancing my career in public health so that I can do more work around the health and wellness of Black people. Black Futures Lab is an organization that serves as a vehicle to build political power for Black people, and they do that through a series of initiatives.[10] The first one was the Black census that was launched back in February 2018. So with the data they were using with the Black census, we are going to use that data to inform policy because the second initiative is the Public Policy Institute. We're developing policies that would improve the lives and conditions of Black people, to restore our dignity, give us power, and transform our communities. As the census is coming to a close, my role will shift a little bit, and I'll be more involved in policy work, which is great because a part of my program is health policy.

I'm learning so much about how things work, and I've met so many people who know all this stuff already and they

---

[10] For more information, see blackfutureslab.org.

probably think it's because they've been doing this work so long but they've had access to institutions or to people who have served as resources for them. I'm a first-generation everything. I am literally building my own framework for what doing this type of work actually means. I went through an organizing training because I understand that, since 2014 and my life changing from this movement and this uprising, this is my life's work. I know that it's going to require formal training in order for me to be the most effective. My life has definitely changed and evolved professionally and politically.

Rev. Tommie Pearson is the pastor of Greater St. Mark Family Church in Ferguson and a former state representative. He also reflects on the losing strategy of "centrism" and the building of Black political power in St. Louis:

I think a lot of eyes have been opened to the importance of African American voters. Claire McCaskill lost. She hadn't done anything for African Americans that I've seen. She didn't even come here during the demonstrations. Now, I know they tried to say that in this last election she did, but that's not true. I was out there. I never saw her. I think too many white Democrats are trying to parade around as Republicans in one place, Democrats in another place trying to make up for the loss of that Black vote because they don't talk to us until election time. But Republicans [are] not going to vote for a fake Republican. And Claire McCaskill learned that the hard way. She paraded around talking about how often she's voted with Donald Trump to please rural white voters, but it did not appeal to African American voters. They asked her on TV, right before the election, if Trump came up for impeachment, would she vote to impeach? She said no. But, doggone, that's the only reason I was voting for her. [laughs] She ain't done nothing else for me. And you ain't going to do that either? So she went down. She went down hard.

So what changes for African Americans? The only change we get is when we make that change ourselves. You take

Andrew Gillum, and you take Stacey Abrams. These are people who carried the ticket. African Americans can carry a ticket standing up for what they believe in. But too many Democrats want to try and appeal to everybody. You are not going to appeal to hardcore Republicans. Trump appeals to them, and they'll never vote for a Democrat in their life. So you can spend all your time trying to get that vote, and you're not going to get it, and you're going to lose some votes that you could get because of that kind of thinking. In my view, a lot of Democrats are trying to play that middle-of-the-road kind of thing, and you've got to stop that. If you're going to take over this country and hold it for a minute, you must be for real. People see that old middle-of-the-road kind of thing and will turn you off in a minute.

African Americans need to establish their own political power. We've got to establish our own political power and turn that into economic power as well because politics and economics go hand-in-hand, and so, when you gain political power, you need to start thinking about economic power too for our communities. We can develop economic development in these communities. These states have a lot of money, and they're spending it someplace else. Why not spend it here? They will go and build a community in a cornfield someplace, and we pay for the infrastructure. And nobody complains about it. Why not develop in these inner cities and inner suburbs? If it's not too expensive to invest out there, it is not too expensive to invest here. It is just a matter of will.

DeMarco Davidson is an Eden Seminary graduate. Here, he reflects on the issue of gun violence and how his dismay propelled him to run for Congress:

When I was in seminary, I took a class on violence, and it was a very tough, challenging class. It was an intensive course—which means it was only three weeks long. We had to do several projects, but because my dad was murdered by gun violence and because of all the different things that were going on in St. Louis, I decided to do a project unpacking gun violence. I wanted to understand more about the factors that influence gun violence, so unpacking the gun violence helped me see that there are at least eight different things that contributed to what I'll call the revolving chamber of gun violence. I believe that until we address these eight different things at once, we will continue to have these issues.

One of the factors involves the Constitution and the way we interpret the Second Amendment. The concept that everybody is supposed to have a gun is not a helpful interpretation. Education levels and poverty are also important factors. I wanted to know more about what our leaders were saying about the gun violence happening in St. Louis and around the country. And I did this project in 2017; so this was before Parkland. This was before Vegas. But I wanted to hear what our leaders were saying about gun violence because St. Louis ranks pretty high.

Our congressperson said, yes, gun violence is a problem, and yes, it is also a public health issue, but we need more police. And he actually was able to get the police —the same police who are not being held accountable for killing unarmed citizens, the same police department that is number one in the country for killing citizens—he was able to get them like $1.5 million. So that also showed me that this current congressperson was able to get funds and resources. And, when I started doing more research on this current congressperson, I was like, well, how long has this person been in office? Oh, since 2000? This is ridiculous.

And what has he done? And where was he during Ferguson? So I began to think "I wonder if someone might be willing to run for Congress?" I worked on Obama's campaign in 2008 and several other campaigns since then. So I went into campaign mode, and the first thing I thought of was what would it take to actually beat this person? So then I looked at who could actually run against him and win. I reached out to certain people, and some just said, nope, they didn't want to do it. Some said, no, they were already planning on running for a different office. And at that time, I was like, you know, if it's going to be, it's up to me.

And, even if I didn't defeat him, I wanted to make sure that people knew that there was somebody who is agitated, who is upset, but, at the same time, focused on providing solutions to some of the problems and some of the issues that…go unnoticed or even unspoken about. So I reached out to several people, sought out wise counsel. Some people were like, "That's going to be extremely challenging." Some people said, "It's going to be impossible." Some people said "Go for it." So I went for it.

Cori Bush leading protest in St. Louis. Eden Seminary President Deb Krause is to her right. *(Photo by Richard Reilly)*

I decided to run for US Congress for the 1st District of Missouri, and it was a blast. I learned so much. I was able to utilize every skill that I had accumulated in the past thirty-plus years of my life. It pushed me to be a better listener. One day, I was having a devotional, and I said to myself *I'm going to be a voice for the voiceless.* And I felt like I heard a voice that said "No. The voiceless *have* a voice. People are just not listening to them. We don't need you to be a voice for the voiceless. We need you to be a listener to those who are not being heard. We need you to see people who are not being seen." After traveling to different churches, going to different neighborhoods and into different communities, I just saw so much pain and suffering. There were times that I would go and knock on a door of a possible voter whose house looked abandoned, and I would say to myself *No one could possibly live here. Please let no one live here.* And somebody would come to the door, and it would just blow me away.

One time, I went to a high school and talked to a group of young male African American students. I asked them about their thoughts on gun violence and how they think we should respond. They said "There are too many guns on the streets. It's not enough for us to do here. We don't know how to deal with this. We don't know how to deal with the anger." Not once did they ever say that we need more police. As I listened to the young people who are living in these communities and neighborhoods, I [became] clear that they know what they want. They know what they need. People know what they need in order to live. Soon afterward I decided to bow out of the race and support another candidate who had garnered a lot of momentum. I thought I was going to relax and take some time off to recuperate, but two days later I receive a call to work on Wesley Bell's campaign.

The candidate that DeMarco began to support was Cori Bush. Bush is a shining example of a St. Louis politician who did not take a "middle-of the-road" stance but instead offered a clear and committed agenda that prioritized the needs of her most vulnerable constituents. She won the 2020 election for Missouri's First Congressional District and unseated longtime incumbent Lacy Clay. As a nurse and Ferguson activist, she spoke directly to the concerns about issues such as economic insecurity, medical debt and health disparities, racial injustice, and educational disparities. She remained unwavering in her support of the kind of reform efforts and community investments that would lead to a more just and equitable community, and her clearly defined message resonated within her constituents.

SENSORY WORK

Cultivating our sense of awareness to the realities of racial injustice around us is essential to the work of creating a just and equitable society. By "seeing" or becoming aware of the dehumanizing pathways we have traveled throughout this country's history that brought us to this moment—pathways that include but are not limited to the colonization of indigenous peoples, enslavement of Africans for hundreds of years, failed efforts during Reconstruction, lynching, racial discrimination in every facet of our society (work, school, housing, criminal justice, voting, healthcare, etc..) and mass incarceration, will help us "connect the dots" of roads that brought us here.

I invite you to take another look at the US Capitol insurrection and the cries to "Make America Great Again" after exploring the aforementioned pathways.

- What connections do you make between the imagery and actions during the insurrection and our historical routes?
- How do you see the racial justice organizing efforts that have grown out of, or been strengthened by, the Ferguson uprising, in relation to our historical routes and contemporary times?

I encourage you to look for evidence in your own city/town where racial justice-oriented pathways are being forged to help lead us into a more equitable future. If you cannot find any, it might be a sign that it's time to blaze a new trail.

* * *

And what does the LORD require of you? To act justly and to love mercy and to walk humbly with your God. — Micah 6:8 (NIV)

CHAPTER 2

The Fire This Time

August 11, 2017 started as a typical Friday for me with work, shuttling our young boys from place to place, and an assortment of other tasks. Like many people, by Friday I am exhausted, and I had planned to go to bed as early as possible. I also wanted to spend some quiet time reflecting on the beautiful life of my friend and colleague, Rev. Dr. Dale Andrews, whose memorial service was being held the next day in Benton Chapel at Vanderbilt Divinity School in Nashville. After the boys were asleep, I made my way to bed but decided to check the news first. There was a scene unfolding that was difficult to interpret at first, when all of the sudden the images became clear.

White people, mostly college aged men clad in khakis and some women, were streaming onto the campus of the University of Virginia by the hundreds, carrying blazing tiki torches and chanting "White lives matter! White lives matter!...You will not replace us! You will not replace us!...Whose Streets? *Our Streets!* Whose Streets? *Our Streets!*... Blood and Soil! Blood and Soil!... Jews will not replace us! Jews will not replace us!... Death to Antifa! Death to Antifa!... One people, One nation, End Immigration! One people, One nation, End Immigration!"

I jumped out of bed, grabbed my bathrobe (as if I were going somewhere!), and began pacing back and forth, quietly shouting "Oh my God! Oh my God! There's a night ride happening at UVA! Get the Black students to safety! Oh my God!" Remember, one of the favored terror tactics of the Ku Klux Klan was riding into Black neighborhoods at night with lit torches to burn homes and torture and/or kill their residents.[11] One of the torch bearers interviewed that night on campus

---

[11] For more information about the lasting effect of night rides on Black victims, see Kidada E. Williams, "Never Get Over It: Night-Riding's Imprint on African American Victims," in Julian Maxwell Hayter and George R. Goethals, Reconstruction and the Arc of Racial (In)Justice (Northampton, MA: Elgar Publishing, 2018).

gave a very clear explanation as to what they were doing and why. He said, "We're honoring the founding fathers who were white. We're honoring all of the great white men who are being smeared and defamed and torn down."[12] This band of white nationalists was protesting the city's decision to remove the statue of Robert E. Lee. The ongoing removal of Confederate monuments around the country spurred a "Unite the Right" demonstration in Charlottesville that weekend. This replication of a Ku Klux Klan night ride was associated with that effort.

Unite the Right demonstration at the
University of Virginia *(Photo by Hawes Spencer)*

As white nationalists paraded around the campus unimpeded by police, university security, or administrators, they made their way to the St. Paul's Memorial Church where an interfaith assembly of hundreds of clergy and laity had gathered to pray and worship in preparation for their faith witness at the Unite the Right demonstration the next day. Rev. Traci Blackmon, a United Church of Christ executive and leader in the Ferguson movement for racial justice, preached the sermon for the worship service that evening. Afterwards, in an essay for the *St. Louis American* newspaper, she described what happened:

---

[12] Paul Murphy, "White Nationalists Use Tiki Torches to Light up Charlottesville March," CNN, August 8, 2017, https://www.cnn.com/2017/08/12/us/white-nationalists-tiki-torch-march-trnd.

Shortly before the benediction, we were informed that a mob of white supremacists were marching toward the church with lighted torches, and we would not be permitted to leave due to the high probability of assault. We were held hostage inside of the church by this raging mob for approximately 30 minutes....When we were finally allowed and encouraged to quickly leave the church, we were ushered out of side and rear doors into an alley and quickly into cars. As we made our way through the area, I began to weep as I saw masses of mostly young white men, clad in Polos and Oxford button-downs with neatly coiffed hair and many donning "Make America Great Again" caps, filling the streets. My tears were not tears of fear, but tears of mourning. It is a sad moment in our nation—and yet not an unpredictable one given the current social and political tone of this presidential administration. I cried because I recognized this moment, not as an escalation of white supremacy in this nation, but rather as its death rattle. And I know that the dying breaths of white supremacy will be long and arduous and violent. I know that there will be casualties on all sides.[13]

The next day, white nationalist and anti-racism protestors were again present for the Unite the Right demonstration. Anti-racism protestors, many of whom were faith leaders from around the country, stood to bear witness to their faith against these actions of bigotry and hatred. All of the major news networks were reporting from Charlottesville and showing the scenes of Confederate flags and Nazi symbols that appeared to be the trademarks of the Unite the Right coalition. My eyes were glued to the television Saturday morning as I tried to learn about the safety of those in the St. Paul's Church and whether the Black people at the University of Virginia had survived the night of terror.

As I watched Joy Reid broadcast live on MSNBC, Rev. Blackmon emerged on screen for an interview. I was relieved to see that she was

[13] Traci Blackmon, "The Dying Breaths of White Supremacy: Witness to Charlottesville Outlines the Way Forward for Anti-Racists," St. Louis American, September 26, 2017, http://www.stlamerican.com/news/local_news/the-dying-breaths-of-white-supremacy-witness-to-charlottesville-outlines-the-way-for-ward-for-anti/article_b8bdf2c0-82b0-11e7-adfc-7f69a341ce12.html

okay, and I listened intently to her recollection of events from the night before. Then all of the sudden, a man firmly put his arm around her and swooped her off the screen, and she could be heard saying "I gotta go, I gotta go!"[14] I let out such a loud shriek that my husband rushed into the room to see what was wrong. Traci is my friend, and at that moment I didn't know whether she was safe or in serious danger. Thankfully, she remained safe.

But many others did not. Later that day, a white man drove a gray Dodge Challenger car at full speed into a gathered group of anti-racist protestors. Heather Heyer, a thirty-two-year-old white woman from Charlottesville, was killed, and dozens of people were seriously injured.

By this time, Donald Trump had been the president of the United States for eight months. When he was elected in November of 2016, many stood stunned in disbelief and denial. There were stark differences between Trump and his opponent, Hillary Clinton, that clearly demonstrated their commitments and capacities for effective and equitable leadership. The pre-election polls were not projecting a win for Trump, and the Clinton campaign had the Javits Convention Center in New York outfitted for a spectacular victory celebration. Many people anticipated that she was on track to become the first woman president in the history of the United States, but that dream was shattered when Clinton called Trump early the next morning to concede. To add insult to injury, many more people actually voted for Clinton than for Trump. Clinton received 65,853,625 versus 62,985,106 votes for Trump. However, Trump won the Electoral College with 306 to Clinton's 232, which by current law made him the president-elect.

On August 15, three days after the Unite the Right demonstrations in Charlottesville, President Trump held a press conference to talk about an executive order he signed related to infrastructure permitting. During this conference, a reporter asked about some previous remarks he'd made regarding the Charlottesville riots, that there were "very fine people on both sides." He further responded to the criticism of the apparent moral equivalency between white nationalists and anti-racist protestors by saying, "If you look at what I said, you will see that that question was answered perfectly. And I was talking about people that went because they felt very strongly about the monument to Robert E.

---

[14] Joy Reid, "Pastor Pulled to Safety at Charlottesville White Nationalists March," MSNBC (NBCUniversal News Group, August 12, 2017), https://www.msnbc.com/am-joy/watch/pastor-pulled-to-safety-at-charlottesville-white-nationalists-march-1023333955836

Lee, a great general. Whether you like it or not, he was one of the great generals."[15]

The president went on during this press conference to reference the protest that had occurred the night before on the University of Virginia campus, the one with the tiki torches. "There were people in that rally, and I looked the night before," he said. "If you look, they were people protesting very quietly the taking down of the statue of Robert E. Lee."[16] I do not recall this quote receiving a lot of media attention, but we should not let it escape us that the president of the United States saw no problem with white people carrying lit torches into the night while chanting racist slogans, and that he cited it as an example of "protesting very quietly." The president's interpretation of Friday night's events stood in stark contrast to the testimony of people who had to shelter in place inside St. Paul's Memorial Church because of the mob that had gathered outside their doors, as well as many people who watched video of the event.

The stark dichotomy between the president's interpretation of the night ride/blaming "both sides" and others who saw all of the Unite the Right activities as brazen acts of white supremacy illustrates the critical point that we do not see and understand racism in the same way. This perennial problem makes it difficult to become an equitable society because there are many that do not believe that racism exists. They don't "see" it, even when it stares them squarely in the face.

To this day, there are radical differences in how the Ferguson uprising is *seen* and understood. People who lived outside of the St. Louis area were particularly dependent on media accounts and interpretations of what occurred and why it was occurring.

In an effort to help people within her denomination understand more about the context and space in which the uprising occurred, Rev. Julie Taylor, a Unitarian Universalist chaplain and Ferguson activist, decided to take on the role of street reporter in order to dispel myths and give truthful accounts about what was happening. She recounts:

---

[15] Angie Holan and Donald Trump, "PolitiFact - In Context: Donald Trump's 'Very Fine People on Both Sides' Remarks (Transcript)," Politifact, April 26, 2019, https://www.politifact.com/article/2019/apr/26/context-trumps-very-fine-people-both-sides-remarks/

[16] Glenn Kessler, "Analysis | President Trump's False Claim That Counter-protesters Lacked a Permit," The Washington Post (WP Company, August 15, 2018), https://www.washingtonpost.com/news/fact-checker/wp/2017/08/16/president-trumps-false-claim-that-counter-demonstrators-lacked-a-permit.

It was a challenge within our denomination, while the uprising was still happening, trying to get white people within our denomination that were not in the metro area to listen to the real story of what was happening as opposed to what was being televised. It was very difficult. I've been invited to speak at a number of different UU congregations, and at some larger gatherings of ministers and religious educators, and one of the things I wound up doing is I took my little video camera, and I got in the van, and I drove. I narrated a video like a dash cam in Ferguson. I said "Alright, this is what you're going to see. This is the neighborhood. These are the Canfield Apartments. This is where Mike's grandmother lived. This is where he was. Look at how tiny the street is." And I said "And you see that spot on the ground right there? This is where he was murdered. That's where his body lay." I left Canfield Drive and turned on to West Florissant and say "Alright. Right there before you at that next stoplight, that's where the Quick Trip was that burned right there." And that stoplight was kind of one end of the protests and then the light turns, and I make a left onto the five-lane street and say, "And here we are. That McDonald's, you saw that McDonald's a lot, and that's Ferguson Avenue. For the most part, for the months of activity, this is the extent of the Ferguson uprising in terms of protest. It is less than a half mile." And the whole video takes about two-and-a-half minutes. And I said, "You have basically just seen the extent of the protests between August and October. So you've been lied to, to hear that Ferguson burned down."

Truth telling as an act of justice

Truth telling—putting claims in context and replacing myths with facts—is integral to the work of awakening our consciousness about how we see and understand the world around us— especially related to matters of race and racism. Julie made a concerted effort to offer a truthful counter narrative to the "Ferguson burned down" narrative that was pervasive among her constituents. History has taught us that actions taken by Black people or on behalf of Black people for the purpose of racial justice are often negatively framed and exaggerated. Yes, the QuickTrip store burned. But the entire town of Ferguson did not burn. Furthermore, if we are going to *see* and understand this context adequately we must also be willing to ask *"Why* did the QuickTrip burn?"* Yes, a police station in Minneapolis burned after the killing of George Floyd. Yet again we must ask *why* the police station burned and consider *what* we must do to address the injustices that led to these types of public outcries.

Protest outside of the Minneapolis police station after the killing of
George Floyd. Rev. Doug Pagitt, activist, executive director of Vote Common Good
and founder of Solomon's Porch. *(Photo by Rev. Doug Pagitt)*

In an interview with Mike Wallace in 1966, Dr. Martin Luther King, Jr. offered a thought-provoking explanation for the riots that had taken place in Chicago that summer:

> I contend that the cry of "Black power" is, at bottom, a reaction to the reluctance of white power to make the kind of changes necessary to make justice a reality for the Negro. I think that we've got to see that a riot is the language of the unheard. And, what is it that America has failed to hear? It has failed to hear that the economic plight of the Negro poor has worsened over the last few years.[17]

---

[17] Mike Wallace and Martin Luther King, "MLK: A Riot Is the Language of the Unheard," CBS News (CBS Interactive, October 16, 2017), https://www.cbsnews.com/news/mlk-a-riot-is-the-language-of-the-unheard/.

The tense relationship between the Chicago police and many in the African American community on the west side of Chicago reached a boiling point that summer and riots resulted in injuries and deaths. If one considers the notion that a riot is the language of the unheard, King goes on to ask about what our country has failed to hear. Today, if you replaced "Black power" with "Black Lives Matter" within King's quote and replied to his question with "It has failed to hear the economic, policing, educational, health, housing, and criminal justice plight of African Americans," we would likely get closer to the truth about why the QuickTrip burned. We would *see* more clearly.

Dr. Carol Anderson, C.H. Candler Professor of African American Studies at Emory University, also skillfully makes the case for examining the cause of "Black rage" that is exhibited in the burning of a store instead of the source of the unrest. She argues that "white rage" should be the focus for understanding how the laws, policies, and social norms, steeped in racial inequity, have set the stage for visceral outbursts against racial injustice:

> With so much attention focused on the flames, everyone had ignored the logs, the kindling. In some ways, it is easy to see why. White rage is not about visible violence, but rather it works its way through the courts, the legislatures, and a range of government bureaucracies. It wreaks havoc subtly, almost imperceptibly. Too imperceptibly, certainly, for a nation consistently drawn to the spectacular—to what it can see. It's not the Klan. White rage doesn't have to wear sheets, burn crosses, or take to the streets. Working the halls of power, it can achieve its ends far more effectively, far more destructively.[18]

Focusing our collective attention on ways that systemic racial inequality shapes and/or informs our socio-political context and working to eradicate it must replace the fixation on the flames. One organization that is doing so is the Urban League of Metropolitan St. Louis.

The Urban League of Metropolitan St. Louis is a nonprofit organization that has advocated for economic empowerment for more than one hundred years. Shortly after the Ferguson uprising began, the president and CEO Michael McMillian quickly involved the Urban

---

[18] Carol Anderson, *White Rage: The Unspoken Truth of our Racial Divide* (New York: Bloomsbury, 2016), 3.

League in myriad ways. The Urban League of Metropolitan St. Louis banner was spotted at several marches around the Ferguson area, and McMillian marched as well. At the same time, he was working to find tangible ways for the organization to invest further in the Ferguson area.

Ferguson Community Empowerment Center *(Photo by Leah Gunning Francis)*

The outcome was the construction of the Ferguson Community Empowerment Center that opened on the third anniversary of Michael Brown's death (August 9, 2017) on the site of the former QuickTrip building that burned during the Ferguson uprising. *St. Louis Magazine* featured an article describing the center and its purpose:

> Created from a partnership between the Urban League of Metropolitan St. Louis and the Salvation Army, the 13,000-square-foot facility will house the Urban League affiliate's Save Our Sons program, an employment and workforce development program that helps African American men find jobs. It's an initiative that was created in the wake of the Ferguson unrest, after the league's staff asked protestors, "How can we help make things better?" The No. 1 response: jobs.[19]

[19] Sarah Kloepple, "The Ferguson Community Empowerment Center Opens on the Ashes of the Burned-down QuikTrip in Ferguson," St. Louis Magazine, August 9, 2017, https://www.stlmag.com/news/ferguson-community-empowerment-center/.

To Dr. King's and Dr. Anderson's point, we must look again at the reasons for riots that erupt in response to racial injustice. Since 2014, tens of thousands of people have marched peacefully in streets across our country to protest police violence against Black people. But for the few such marches that actually have become "riots," we must do the harder work of looking more closely, asking why, and working to address the cause, and not spend all of our time discussing the symptoms.

Outside of the new Community Empowerment Center rests a bench in honor of Michael Brown, Jr., that includes materials from the former memorial on Canfield Drive, the site of his killing. Rev. Tommie Pierson, pastor of Greater St. Mark Family Church in Ferguson, offered the dedication prayer for the bench during the grand opening activities.

Memorial bench in honor of Michael Brown at the Ferguson Community Empowerment Center *(Photo by Leah Gunning Francis)*

"People saw the need and stepped up"

Greater St. Mark Family Church in Ferguson quickly became a hub for movement activity after Brown was killed. The two most apparent reasons for this are, first, its proximity to the site, and second, the church's willingness to open its doors. Rev. Tommie Pierson was and still is the pastor of that church. When I interviewed him for *Ferguson and Faith*, he recalled being asked by people around the world how the church got involved. He responded:

And this thing just kind of blossomed. I got to church one Sunday and there was a flyer on my windshield, and it was talking about a meeting. And I looked at it, and I said "Wow. This looks pretty good. I think I'm going to try and go to this." And I turned it over, and it was at this church. [*laughs*] And during that time, there were people all over the place. We had meetings up in the sanctuary, meetings at the school, meetings back here, meetings downstairs…And so that's how I got involved. I said "Yes" one time.[20]

While Rev. Pierson acknowledged then that he didn't know all that saying "yes" would mean, when I interviewed him again for this follow-up book, he was able to gauge the impact of the past several years. His reflections revealed some of the challenges that emerged during the protests:

I had several members in the church that actually were involved with the protests. Some perhaps were more involved than I knew. It wasn't until later that I knew several of them were involved because they shared with me that the word on the street down there is that, if you get scratched, hurt, maced, teargassed, go to Greater St. Mark's. I didn't know that, and that's what they did. We had stuff here for them to treat their eyes or a Band-Aid or grab a sandwich and a soda, some water, something like that. And, fortunately, we had sociologists and psychologists who actually started coming to church every Sunday just in case somebody needed their services. The things that we needed were here for the church and for anyone else who came. And I didn't invite anyone because I was caught up in what was going on. It's just that people saw the need and stepped up. They just showed up.

And as I think about how this has impacted me, I'm just glad that God put me in this space when he did so that I could play a role in terms of space for the protestors and everybody who wanted to have a voice in what was going on. And how it has impacted me since then is it was a big struggle for me that I never really talked about because we had just acquired the mortgage on this property, and we had no money. And so, when all the people started coming, it became a challenge for the church. We had to sit down and

---

[20] Pearson, *Ferguson and Faith*, 31.

make a decision as to how we were going to get through this. So I shared with the church that, whatever happens, we're going to pay the mortgage. If the utilities get shut off, we can get them back on at a later date. We're going to pay the mortgage because, if they foreclose on us, then we really have an issue. We've got a problem. And that's what we did. But fortunately, some other people saw that and recognized the need of the church, like unions, social groups, and individuals began to make contributions which saved us. I did not want to place a burden on the church. All the things that I went through, I went through it. I didn't involve the church and—because I've been around long enough to know that, if you place that kind of burden on individuals in the church, they put the pressure back on you that you've got to stop or we're leaving kind of thing. And we did lose some members, but, fortunately, we didn't lose very many.

And I never will forget there was a young African American woman who lived in South St. Louis. She called me up, and she said, "Reverend, I want to give a donation to the church." We tried for two or three weeks to connect, but she [finally] came here and brought a check. And I didn't have my glasses on. I looked at the check. I just glanced at it, and it looked like $15 to me. When I came back and put my glasses on, it was $1,500. Well, I wanted to catch her [laughs], but it was too late.

It was people like that that renewed my faith and my hope. She just saw it on the news and decided she would make a contribution. So that was great. There were people out of town who would send $20, $25, stuff like that. It was a great experience for me and for the church because I would share everything that went down like that, I would share with the church. These are the things that happened as a result of what we were doing as a church by providing this space for people. This is what was happening behind the scenes.

Doing the work of racial justice is largely "behind the scenes" work. Whenever we see an organized march, rally, or protest, there has been a significant amount time and energy that has gone into planning and executing the event. Beyond the protests, there are groups and organizations that are combatting racial injustice and advocating for racial equity on a daily basis in areas such as healthcare, law, criminal justice, education, environment and housing—to name a few. For example, the Deaconess Foundation, a philanthropic ministry of the United Church of Christ in St. Louis, focuses their grant-making initiatives on child well-being in the St. Louis region. Their vision statement articulates the kind of community they seek to help build:

> Deaconess Foundation envisions a community that values the health and well-being of all children and gives priority attention to the most vulnerable. This community only thrives if the allocation of power and distribution of resources, benefits, opportunities and burdens are not predictable by, nor predicated on race.[21]

Rev. Dr. Starsky Wilson was the president and CEO of the Deaconess Foundation from 2011 to 2020 and provided exemplary leadership for fulfilling the organization's mission and vision to prioritize the well-being of St. Louis area children who were most in need. Dr. Wilson's unwavering commitment to child well-being and racial justice is respected throughout the philanthropic and advocacy communities, and in September 2020 he became the president and CEO of the Children's Defense Fund in Washington, DC. However, Deaconess Foundation continues to fulfill its mission and vision and is well-situated to carry on the work of racial equality that was largely initiated by Dr. Wilson.

Rev. Willis Johnson was the pastor of Wellspring United Methodist Church in Ferguson. The church was located near the Ferguson police station and was also a major hub of activity during the Ferguson uprising. Since that time, he has published a book titled *Holding Up Your Corner: Talking about Race in Your Community*, in which he gives practical guidance for pastors and congregations for talking about race and responding to issues of racial injustice:[22]

---

[21] "Mission, Vision & Values," Deaconess Foundation, June 23, 2020, https://deaconess.org/mission-vision-values/.

[22] F. Willis Johnson, *Holding Up Your Corner: Talking about Race in Your Community* (Nashville, TN: Abingdon Press, 2017).

In the summer of 2018, my family and I relocated from Ferguson to Columbus, Ohio, to do a similar work of starting a new faith community, planning a church from the ground up, or doing what they call in the business a "parachute plan." Still in the United Methodist faith tradition but in a little bit [of a] different context.

But, interestingly,... Columbus over the last year has had a series of civilian police encounters, even one fatal shooting. And so we left the city but not the situation. And so my work continues.

I published a book that came out in 2016 [in which] I was invited to share about some of our work and perspective on leading and living in Ferguson, and really [the publisher] wanted me to chronicle what it was like and what happened. I took the opportunity to talk about what does it mean as a faith leader, as a practitioner to begin to process and orientate oneself in light of the inevitable, which is our faith in crisis, and used the backdrop of the situations in Ferguson along with other forms of injustice and highlighted the fact that there's a systemic and historical practice of othering and of being disingenuous and inhumane, and that that is antithetical to my faith understanding.

And so, [as a] practitioner of faith it is incumbent upon us to be ready and to be willing to act, and not wait for something to happen but be in process, be in practice, be in a way of justice ministry. Before August 9, 2014, Wellspring Church was there. After sometime in August 2014, Wellspring Church was still there. And what we were able to do or what we tried to do was to hold up our little corner in Ferguson.

Wellspring looked like much of Ferguson. We were tracking for a church plan, we were heading towards our apex. We were just short of about three-and-a-half years at that point. And so it was a pretty healthy place and growing place and getting good traction. In general, probably the easiest way to summarize [what happened next] is that— as a small community within the community—we got overwhelmed. Personally and collectively.

> We went from a little church in a big building to a little church that had a mega ministering expectation and responsibility. Their pastor became something else. There were cameras in the sanctuary every Sunday. I mean, for a year, there were cameras from around the world. I've got clippings and video clips in languages I can't even identify. We just became more than the church. We became a lot of things that, as a newly established church, most people don't sign on for. They didn't sign on to become an activist space. They didn't sign up for it and as my wife told me one Sunday after a month of Sundays "Can we not talk about Ferguson?" We didn't just drive in, we lived there. So for most people, it just became—it was overwhelming.

Truth telling remains an essential virtue for building roads that will lead us into a future filled with hope. There were financial and emotional costs for many of the congregations and individuals who engaged in this work. The risk of things not turning out exactly as planned is not unusual, as with in life in general. Standing in our truth and being willing to assess where we are to determine the next best steps is an ongoing process.

The Stockley Verdict

One of the truths that remained after the Ferguson uprising is that the concerns about police violence against Black people did not go away. The timeline at the beginning of this book names just a few of the Black people whom police have killed since Michael Brown. One of the largest protests that occurred in St. Louis after Ferguson followed the acquittal of police officer Jason Stockley on September 15, 2017. Rev. David Gerth, executive director of Metropolitan Congregations United (MCU), and the MCU staff led or helped coordinate many clergy-related actions during the Ferguson uprising. Below, Rev. Gerth recalls his experience of the being part of the Stockley verdict protests:

> One of the biggest impacts, I would say, has been what happened with the Stockley verdict. The Stockley verdict would have been a whole different thing, I think, if we hadn't had our Mike Brown Ferguson experience. Stockley was a St. Louis City police officer who was responsible for killing

Anthony Lamar Smith in 2011, before Mike Brown was killed. I suppose people noticed at the time, but the trial was in 2017, and everybody was watching the trial very closely. It seemed pretty clear that Stockley was recorded on his radio saying that he was going to kill the guy who was driving the car he was chasing. And it also seemed pretty clear that he planted the gun in Anthony Lamar Smith's car that gave him the cover to say that he feared for his life and that the man was armed. Last year, people started anticipating the decision. It was a bench trial. They decided not to have a jury trial, so it was up to a judge. We all thought that maybe that meant there was a better chance that he would be held accountable in some way, and we began trying to decide whether we were going to be involved as an organization. Some of the folks we were close to were doing some things, and we started going along. By the time it looked like there was going to be a decision, we had actually started organizing congregations again to provide safe space.

The judge's decision was announced on a Friday night, and there was a very large demonstration not far from our office, up and down Kings Highway and up and down the streets in the Central West End. There were three- to five-thousand people on a Friday night, and we had lined up five churches that would be available as safe spaces if they were needed, but by 9:00 or so, the protest was officially ending, and a lot of people left. But some folks ended up at the mayor's house, and there was some damage done to her house, and things really escalated badly from there. There was teargas and rubber bullets and the whole nine yards. Police pushed protestors up Waterman Ave. toward Central Reform Church and First Unitarian, both of which were places that we had set up with food and water. People went into those places seeking refuge, and the police then tried to occupy those spaces and released teargas. So we ended up spending the rest of the night all over the Central West End. Police released teargas all over the neighborhood, on private streets, all the way up here by Trinity Episcopal, which was one of our other safe spaces.

Protests after the Stockley verdict in St. Louis
and the police in riot gear *(Photos by David Gerth)*

For me personally, it was a little bit like the Ferguson
experience. It's one thing to watch it. It's another thing to
even go to a rally or a march. It's another thing [altogether]
to see the force of the police whom we pay being deployed
against us. At MCU, we had built a campaign out of our
Ferguson experience around the school-to-prison pipeline
and had decided we were going to keep ourselves focused

on that campaign. However, there were a number of us out in these protests in clergy gear with the hopes of helping modulate the impact of the use of force by the police.

Stockley protest outside of police headquarters.
September 2017 *(Photo by David Gerth)*

During one Stockley protest, two clergy were standing at the back of the march to make sure that the intersections were secure as the last of the marchers made it through. There were police who came and put their hands on these two clergy and raised their voices and said, "You need to get out of here. We're in charge of this corner." And the clergy said, "We're just trying to make sure that everybody is getting through here safely." And then a third clergy person came over and—because that person could see what was going on—said [to the police], "Please step away from these other two." And that person was thrown on the ground with a police officer's knee in that person's back, handcuffed, and dragged away. The person lost their glasses and said, "Could you get my glasses for me?" and an officer walked over and smashed them. While that was happening, everything escalated around so there's no modulating. There's no toning down by the police at all. In fact there's escalation possibly because it's clergy at that point. I'm not saying that they don't escalate more with other people, but it seemed that was bugging them, and so one of the protestors was moving away and was tasered and then maced. This is actually very dangerous because the intersection between the material that they use for the mace and the electrical charge [from the taser] can actually ignite, so it's counter to procedure. I've seen people maced and teargassed, but I've never seen worse than that night.

Stockley protest outside of Cardinals' game.
September 2017*(Photo by David Gerth)*

It was very discouraging because that was under the leadership of a relatively new mayor. That was kind of her first demonstration of what was going to happen under her administration. We had several weeks of other kinds of experiences. Some better, some worse. Once . . . the police were in their full riot gear and had their nightsticks, and I just thought, between the pepper spray and the nightsticks, we're all in a lot of trouble. There were a couple of people who were whacked with nightsticks and, I think, had some minor injuries, but it was not as nearly as bad as I [had feared]. Most people, as we were arrested, were treated procedurally the way that you would expect. Things were done appropriately. But when the officers came and picked me up, the officer put the ties on my wrist. There were people who could actually slide out of their ties, sort of like a civil disobedience arrest where everybody's going to have to go through the procedure, but everybody's being treated with a lot of respect. But the officer who put my twist ties on, he got a hold of my wrist and just cranked that thing down as hard as he could right on that joint. It's still a little tender there, and I wasn't actually sure if he was really doing serious damage to my body because of the way that was on there. There were a couple of other people who had them cranked down like that too.

There is something diseased in someone's experience that they were looking for an opportunity to inflict pain. If they're willing to do that then, what are they willing to do when there's not a TV camera watching? It's an illness that exists within our system of policing. I think for officers who start out for the right reasons and try to keep going for the right reasons, they are swimming upstream.

Jia Lian Yang, an Eden Seminary graduate and activist, gives a similar account of excessive force that was used during the Stockley protests. (When I interviewed her for *Ferguson and Faith*, she was identified as Karen Yang but has since decided to be identified by her Chinese birth name, Jia Lian. She will talk more about this in a later chapter.) Here she talks about Stockley:

When the Stockley verdict came down, a lot of people in St. Louis came out because of the non-indictment. We saw the same kind of theater happen again when barrier fences went up around City Hall and the police headquarters. I went out the very first day that the non-indictment came out and was immediately pepper-sprayed by police and had bikes rammed into me so that I had bruises because we were standing in the street. They turned our public transportation, Metro Buses, into riot buses because they filled them with riot police head-to-toe in SWAT gear. The bike cops weaponized their bikes, which you think, in the city, that's what they use to get around. Instead, they used those to ram protestors.

Rev. Gerth continues his reflection on what he sees has changed related to the protests since the Ferguson uprising:

> One of the things that changed because of Ferguson is that we are a community that has the capacity to lead the kind actions that don't need to have a central driving force. It can be very organic from multiple different directions. And I think what happened in the Stockley verdict response was that there was pretty good coordination. There's always tension in protest movements, but there was pretty good coordination. And a lot of that was from people who had learned lessons not just about how to conduct an effective protest but how to work together even when there's a lot of tension. There was plenty of tension, but it rarely stopped people from working effectively together.

Rabbi Susan Talve reflects on the role that her congregation, Central Reform Congregation, played during the Stockley protests in providing safe sanctuary and on the cultural shift that began to happen after Ferguson:

> When the protests happened after the Stockley verdict, we welcomed the protestors. I went out and said to the police, "These are our guests and we'll keep them safe." The police had surrounded the building, and I went back inside and said "Don't leave until they tell you it's safe. Stay here. We can keep you safe." And we did until about one in the morning. I was grateful that we were prepared to welcome family in.
>
> That night we saw how different the protest community looked. It was much more diverse. Something happened in those four years. Something happened that grew the movement. It grew the movement. We'd said so many times that when you care more about property damage than you do life, that's idolatry. We'd said that so many times that it had become a mantra, and people understood that. Even when shop owners on Delmar and different places had their windows broken, they'd said, "We can

fix our windows. We can't bring back a life." People had gotten that mantra. We had shifted the culture just a little bit over those years.

Then the nation voted in an administration that is getting away with growing white supremacy and white nationalism, that is giving permission to people who are against immigration to go and shoot a synagogue. The people who were killed at the Louisville Kroger, they were killed because someone couldn't get into a church. It's the same root of hate. It's the same root of ignorance. It's the same root of using fear and hate speech to divide people. Our only response can be to love each other more in word and deed.

It's not about arming each other more. The guy in Thousand Oaks shot the guards first. More guns mean more killing. It's [time to] ban the assault rifles, get rid of the bump stocks—anything that makes it easier to kill because this is about mass killing. And what our administration is doing is giving permission to take that hate speech and make it hate deed.

SENSORY WORK

Throughout history, we have seen fits of rage result in fires. For centuries, white supremacists have burned Black people's homes, businesses, churches, and bodies as a terroristic tactic to prevent or punish Black people's pursuit of equal citizenship. More recently, in response to the racial injustice that has been inflicted through police violence, we saw the Quick Trip burn in Ferguson and a Minneapolis police station burn after George Floyd was killed.

I invite you to consider Dr. King's words in this chapter on riots in response to racial injustice.

- What are the flames in Ferguson and Minneapolis telling us about racial injustice?
- To whose cries haven't we been listening and why?

I encourage you bring your entire being into this work and consider ways to engage in an ongoing practice of listening to the truths of those who have suffered racial discrimination.

- How might these truths guide our processes for forging new pathways toward a racially just and equitable society?

* * *

Truth is nowhere to be found, and whoever shuns evil becomes a prey. The LORD looked and was displeased that there was no justice. — *Isaiah 59:15 (NIV)*

CHAPTER 3

·······················

Words Create Worlds

For four consecutive years, a steady stream of name-calling, insults, derogatory attacks, and lies have flooded the airwaves. One might imagine that these indignities only emerged from music with warning labels or "shock jocks" who go too far. But no, they came from the president of the United States during press conferences, interviews, Make American Great Again (MAGA) rallies, and through social media posts. His lies and incendiary rhetoric were staples on his Twitter account long before his presidential run.

For example, he promulgated what came to be known as the "birther" movement when, throughout the Obama presidency, he insisted that President Obama was lying about his birthplace, and he was not in fact an American citizen. Trump spread these lies for years and only switched subjects when he became president in 2016.

The documented lies and insults continued throughout his entire presidency.[23] His targets were anyone who questioned his actions and intentions or disagreed with him. He regularly called the news media (with the exception of Fox News) "fake news" and demeaned journalists at every opportunity. While he insulted men and women of a variety of races, he had a particular cadence to his insult of Black people. Black politicians, journalists, and athletes he regularly mocked for having a "low-IQ" (Congresswoman Maxine Waters), for being a "loser" (White House correspondent April Ryan), "stupid" (CNN journalist Abby Phillip), and "dumb" (CNN anchor Don Lemon).

Insulting Black people's intelligence is a long-standing racist trope. The white supremacist movement has long worked to deem Black

---

[23] Glen Kessler, "Analysis | Tracking All of President Trump's False or Misleading Claims," The Washington Post (WP Company, January 20, 2021), https://www.washingtonpost.com/graphics/politics/trump-claims-database/

people inferior to white people, including intellectually inferior. Our capacities for intellectual rigor are challenged in academic spaces, as is our competency in professional spaces.[24] During a press conference on March 29, 2020, President Trump never even gave White House Correspondent for PBS News Hour Yamiche Alcindor a chance to ask her question before he launched a full-throated insult:

Trump: "Why don't you act in a little more positive …"
Alcindor: "My question to you is …"
Trump: "It's always …getcha, getcha … And you know what? That's why nobody trusts the media anymore …"
Alcindor: "My question to you is how is this going to impact …"
Trump: "Excuse me. You didn't hear me. That's why you used to work for the *Times* and now you work for someone else. Look, let me tell you something: Be nice …"
Alcindor: "Mr. President, my question is …"
Trump: "Don't be threatening. Be nice. Go ahead."[25]

He never even gave her an opportunity to ask her question. Yes, this is a thinly veiled attempt not to have to answer a journalist's question and deflect from the issue that was being pursued. However, it also profoundly abusive, unprofessional, and hurtful.

The president of the United States on a regular basis mocked and demeaned Ms. Alcindor, a Black woman, for doing her job—actually merely for *existing*. There are workplace laws that are supposed to prevent this type of abuse in the workplace. However, when the "boss" is the president of the United States, EEOC laws apparently do not apply.

When Colin Kaepernick, former quarterback for the San Francisco 49ers, quietly kneeled during the playing of the National Anthem on September 1, 2016, he did so to protest the ongoing police brutality against Black people.

Recall: Earlier that summer, police killed Alton Sterling in Louisiana while he was selling CDs in front of a Baton Rouge store; police killed Philando Castile in his car in Minnesota after pulling him

---

[24] Gabriella Gutierrez y Muhs, Yolanda Flores Niemann, Carmen G. Gonzalez and Angela P. Harris, eds. Presumed Incompetent: The Intersections of Race and Class for Women in Academia (Boulder: University of Colorado Press, 2012).

[25] Ricardo Sandoval-Palos, "The Nasty Truth," PBS (Public Broadcasting Service, April 14, 2020), https://www.pbs.org/publiceditor/blogs/pbs-public-editor/the-nasty-truth/

over, shooting him to death in front of his girlfriend and her young daughter; and police shot Charles Kinsey, a mental health therapist, in the leg in Florida while he was lying on his back with his hands up as he tried to talk his autistic patient into going back to the group home; and the police were acquitted of killing Freddie Gray in Baltimore.

Kaepernick's form of protest started picking up steam and other players on other teams started kneeling during the anthem as well. However, President Trump began to frame the protest as "disrespecting the flag" as opposed to protesting police violence. During one of his MAGA rallies in Alabama in 2017, President Trump went so far as to call these players a "son of a bitch" as he stood behind the podium affixed with the presidential seal.[26] In short, his vulgar words had the full weight and support of the United States government in that moment and beyond.

I was incensed when I saw the video clip. As a country, we had devolved to tolerating this kind of tyrannical behavior from the person who was supposed to be the president of all of us. I knew that if one of my sons went to school and called his teacher or classmates a "son of a bitch," he would immediately be suspended or possibly expelled. However, we tolerated the president of the United States calling US citizens "a son of a bitch," as they tried to get police officers to stop killing unarmed Black people. In other words, we were holding our fifth graders to a higher moral and ethical standard than the president of the United States.

"Words create worlds," said Rabbi Abraham Heschel, esteemed theologian and human rights advocate. Dr. Heschel's daughter, Susannah, writes about her father's insistence on speaking with care:

> Words, he often wrote, are themselves sacred, God's tool for creating the universe, and our tools for bringing holiness or evil into the world. He used to remind us [that] the holocaust did not begin with the building of crematoria, with tanks and guns. It began with the uttering of evil words, with defamation, with language and propaganda. Words create worlds, he used to tell me when I was a child. They must be used very carefully. Some words, once having been uttered,

---

[26] Aric Jenkins, "This Is Everything Donald Trump Said in His NFL Speech," Time (Time, September 23, 2017), https://time.com/4954684/donald-trump-nfl-speech-anthem-protests/

gain eternity and can never be withdrawn. The book of Proverbs reminds us, he wrote, that death and life are in the power of the tongue.[27]

Toni Cade Bambara, a renowned author, professor, and civil rights activist, also wrote passionately about the power of words.

> Words are to be taken seriously. I try to take seriously acts of language. Words set things in motion. I've seen them doing it. Words set up atmospheres, electrical fields, charges. I've felt them doing it. Words conjure. I try not to be careless about what I utter, write, sing. I'm careful about what I give voice to.[28]

We must take seriously the impact of words on our minds, bodies, and spirits. When the faulty sticks and stones logic emerges, we are often expected simply to shake off the harmful words and move on. This is a terrible strategy for healing from the word-wounds of this former administration.

We do not have the luxury of saying, "Well, that was then; this is now." Part of the challenge that we face in trying to address racial injustice is an unwillingness to acknowledge, or the impulse to quickly move past, the trauma that has occurred. It was traumatic to hear people dehumanized on a regular basis by the president and many staffers whom our tax dollars paid to work on behalf of all of the people of the United States.

Furthermore, the hate speech promulgated by the president became normalized because it was continuously spewed *without consequence*. Our justice work must include reconstituting new social norms for acceptable rules of engagement that denounce that type of violent rhetoric and call for a higher moral and ethical standard of leadership.

Rabbi Susan Talve has been a stalwart on the frontlines for justice causes in St. Louis for more than thirty years. The founding rabbi of

---

[27] Susannah Heschel, ed., Moral Grandeur and Spiritual Audacity: Essays (New York: Farrer, Straus and Giroux, 1997).

[28] Toni Cade Bambara, "What It Is I Think I'm Doing Anyhow," The Writer on Her Work, edited by Janet Sternburg (New York: W.W. Norton and Company, 1980), 163.

Central Reform Congregation in St. Louis, she reflects on the years since the Ferguson uprising and the impact of the hate speech:

> Ferguson happened here. The fires burned here, but it wasn't just about here. It had to be in the heartland of America to show that it's all over America, and we can't hide. There's no hiding from the violence that was the murder of Mike Brown. The violence that was the murder of VonDerrit Myers. The violence that was the murder of unarmed Black men and kids who were mercilessly profiled. It uncovered a sickness in this nation that has challenged us to choose how to respond. Some have responded with fear and with believing this is something you can take sides on. And there are those of us who know that this is not about sides. This is about family. This is about seeing humanity in everyone and knowing that no child is safe until all children are safe.
>
> We passed progressive amendments that raise the minimum wage and vote for a Clean Missouri, which is good. Hopefully, new marijuana laws will help with our terrible mass incarceration problem [...] and not target people who can least afford it. But until we take care of the bail bond system, until we really get the training for our police that we need to un-militarize, we are complicit. And as long as we continue to support an administration that gets away with hate speech that leads to hate action, we are complicit. When we continue to support an administration that is all about division and not about seeing the humanity in every person but dares to demonize the other, dares to demonize the caravan of people who are coming from Honduras, Guatemala, El Salvador, Nicaragua, and Mexico—these thousands of people who have risked everything to save their lives and the lives of their children and grandchildren—if we dare to demonize them, we've lost everything. We've lost hope, and Mike died in vain. What we came to understand on the streets of Ferguson was that we could not let Mike Brown die in vain. We had to change things, and it wasn't just Mike. It was every child that was a victim of a system that would criminalize our children.

The Holy Family in detainment on the lawn of Christ Church Cathedral
in Indianapolis in 2018. *(Photo by Rev. Steve Carlsen)*

The Holy Family in detainment on the lawn of Christ Church Cathedral
in Indianapolis in 2018. *(Photo by Rev. Steve Carlsen)*

The immigration crisis that emerged in 2018 along the southern US
border was framed and often justified by the dehumanizing rhetoric of
the president and his staff that characterized people most often seeking

asylum as rapists and murders. These negative stereotypes he used to try and sway public opinion toward justifying the harsh treatment asylum seekers received after entering the US. As word spread of families being separated and detained in inhumane conditions, such as children sleeping on cold floors under aluminum blankets and insufficient food and medical services, protests starting forming in cities around the country.

In Indianapolis, where I live, a local church took their protest to a new level: They put Mary, Joseph, and baby Jesus in a cage on the church lawn. Rev. Lee Curtis, who served as Canon Missioner at Christ Church Cathedral, came up with the idea and worked with Rev. Steve Carlsen, who served as dean and rector, to orchestrate the display and create the #EveryFamilyisHoly campaign. They wanted to send the message that Jesus's family once sought asylum from an unjust regime and that we ought to honor the humanity of today's asylum seekers as a holy families too. It was the most righteous display of solidarity I have ever seen on a church lawn.

Rabbi Talve describes her reasoning for engaging in the protests.

> And the truth is, the reason that I had to be there on the streets of Ferguson and I have to find a way to continue to be in this fight is, number one, because I really love my friends, and I'm going to stand. That's who my family is. I'm going to stand with my family when they're at risk. And, oh my God, have I found after the Tree of Life mass shooting in Pittsburgh, how I'm not standing alone either. More people have shown up for us and said "We've got your back." Almost every member of the African American community that was part of the protest community either called or texted me with those words "We've got your back. We've got your back, sister." It meant more to me than I could say.

On October 27, 2018, a forty-six year-old white man shot and killed eleven people during a Shabbat morning service at the Tree of Life Synagogue in Pittsburgh, Pennsylvania. The shooter had allegedly posted anti-Semitic comments on various social media sites prior to what is known as the worst attack on a Jewish community in United States history. These are the names and ages of the eleven people who were killed in this attack:

> *Joyce Fienberg, 75*
>
> *Richard Gottfried, 65*
>
> *Rose Mallinger, 97*
>
> *Jerry Rabinowitz, 66*
>
> *Cecil Rosenthal, 59*
>
> *David Rosenthal, 54*
>
> *Bernice Simon, 84*
>
> *Sylvan Simon, 86*
>
> *Daniel Stein, 71*
>
> *Melvin Wax, 88*
>
> *Irving Younger, 69*

Rabbi Talve continues her reflections:

The other reason I felt I had to be on the streets of Ferguson and continue to find a way to be involved is because this is about all of us. Whenever anyone is marginalized, we're all at risk. It's just convenience that maybe it's one group today or another tomorrow, but we're all at risk. Nobody is safe. It's an illusion to think that anybody who doesn't fit the white nationalist ideology can hide. Nobody hides. The only response is not to play their game, not to do to them what they've done to us. The only response is to grow family.

Everything we do today has to be to respond with love and not out of fear. But when you have a nation that continues to support an administration that is getting away with supporting white supremacy, and when you really begin to understand that this movement of white nationalism is really antisemitism. The theory of white nationalism is exactly what happened in Nazi Germany, and of course, it's about racism as it turns the Jews into a race, which is what Hitler did. He turned us into a race of people while we are many races as Jews. It erases Black Jews and turns white Jews, whether they like it or not, into a dehumanized group of people. It's happened many time in the story of my people. We get into a position of comfort where we are, and we forget. We forget how vulnerable we are.

#WhiteChurchQuiet?

While Christ Church Cathedral in Indianapolis, a predominately white church, along with other congregations around the country have engaged in acts of racial justice, they are not the norm. There has been a significant amount of criticism of many white churches remaining silent in the wake of racial injustice. Rev. Dr. Andre Johnson, associate professor of Communication, Rhetoric, Race, Religion, Media, and African American Public Address at the University of Memphis and the pastor of Gifts of Life Ministries, started the #WhiteChurchQuiet hashtag on social media to try and generate conversation about this glaring silence. During a lecture at Loyola University–Maryland in 2017, Dr. Johnson described his quest to try and learn more about what was happening in white churches in the midst of recurring instances of police violence against Black people:

Candlelight vigil in the Shaw neighborhood in
St. Louis for the third anniversary of VonDerrit Myers's death.
October 8, 2017. *(Photo by David Gerth)*

> To find the answers that I was in search for, I took to Twitter and started the #WhiteChurchQuiet hashtag. I started it because I wanted to hear from members of predominate[ly] white churches and get their reasoning behind the silence. I wanted to know what pastors and preachers were saying when yet another Black person is shot and killed. I wanted to know how many, who already celebrate law enforcement on a regular basis, would also stand with the victims of police brutality. I wanted to know if they mentioned Black Lives Matter in white churches and if so how was it mentioned.[29]

Dr. Johnson went on to talk about the kind of responses and rationales he received. While some wrote about their efforts to work toward dismantling racism, most reported that their church leaders did not speak out against the police violence against Black people. They most often cited fear as a reason; however, there is also the reality that many do not believe such violence to be an injustice.

Rev. Michelle Higgins is the co-chair of Action St. Louis. She reflects on her experience as a Black Evangelical, and the challenge of engaging her faith community in the movement for racial justice in St. Louis:

> Kayla Reed, one of the Ferguson protestors who was on the frontlines there in Ferguson, and I run what is now Action St. Louis. We have two standing campaigns: political involvement, which is electoral justice as a tool for Black liberation, and an end of prisons. We are prison and police abolitionists, and right now, [we] are seeking to close the Workhouse which is the local medium-security institution in St. Louis. So our campaigns involve police brutality, mass incarceration, and the political process as electoral justice.

---

[29] Andre E. Johnson, "White Silence and the Making of #WhiteChurch-Quiet," Rhetoric Race and Religion (Patheos Explore the world's faith through different perspectives on religion and spirituality! Patheos has the views of the prevalent religions and spiritualities of the world., April 12, 2017), https://www.patheos.com/blogs/rhetoricraceandreligion/2017/04/white-silence-and-the-making-of-whitechurchquiet.html.

For me, the big explosion was VonDerrit Myers. He was murdered a few blocks from my church in the Shaw neighborhood of St. Louis, and I was already marching, had already been connected to a number of the activists in Ferguson. But VonDerrit's murder, and subsequently meeting, getting to know, and befriending VonDerrit's parents, really shook me. And, sadly, I looked around the faith communities that I'm from, the Evangelical faith community, and nobody cared. Maybe twelve of the people that I got in touch with who identify as Evangelicals, there were just maybe a dozen of us in St. Louis —and many more across the country. We had about a dozen people that I was with in 2014 and especially after VonDerrit's murder in October of 2014. During that time, I founded Faith for Justice, which is the Evangelical progressive [organization] that promotes the idea is that communities of faith that identify as Evangelical should be the first to support and to promote the Movement for Black Lives.

In the city of St. Louis, people who believe that their faith is at odds with the Movement for Black Lives might come to a Faith for Justice meeting rather than bringing their fear, arrogance, presumptuousness, or sincere trepidation directly to an Action St. Louis meeting. So you come to Faith for Justice. You get trained. We encounter whatever [*laughs*] stuff that people of faith bring like Christian privilege. We take care of that and then we move them into movement work. And part of what brought me into movement work overall is the belief that there were so many Evangelicals who thought they knew everything, and they realized, I don't know anything; so they just gave up.

I think Black radicalism is scary to Evangelicals, and I believe that Black power is something that, despite the fact that the Almighty God that we worship has kernels of truth in most every liberation movement—I mean liberation is seeking the way of God because truth sets you free. That's what Jesus said. Despite that, Evangelicalism is so corrupted by white supremacy that, when people encounter a truth from non-Christians—the Movement for Black Lives is overwhelmingly "secular"—and they're speaking real truth. And so when Evangelicals, who too often think they own the truth, encounter that truth, they were so shocked. They didn't know what to do with it. They didn't know how to enter in, and many that I was able to speak to admitted "I was terrified because I thought they know more about freedom than me and my Christian self, and it scared me to wonder am I really worshipping Jesus." And so that's what made me determined to push forward, to keep going because I knew that's where the Holy Spirit was leading me, was leading me to be a servant to the Movement for Black Lives, and that is, in my estimation, serving God just as much as my job as like a worship leader. I lead music, and I write books and articles, and I do podcasts and write songs and stuff. It's the all the same for me.

The Racialized Imagination

In a short essay that I wrote a few months after Michael Brown was killed in Ferguson, titled "A Boy, A Wrestler, and the Racialized Imagination," I recounted my struggle with trying to understand why a grand jury would believe that an unarmed eighteen-year-old would run toward the man who is shooting at him. *Nobody would believe that,* I thought to myself as the grand jury deliberated the officer's fate. The officer testified to the grand jury that he felt "like a five-year-old holding onto Hulk Hogan....with demon eyes...that's just how big he felt and how small I felt just from grasping his arm," as he recounted the alleged struggle before he began shooting Brown. He went on to describe how, after he shot Michael in the arm several times, Michael began "charging" toward him, and that is when the officer fired the final and fatal shots to Michael's head.

The officer and Michael Brown were approximately the same height. Witnesses say that Brown had his hands up and started falling forward after being shot multiple times in the arm, not "charging" the officer. However, the jury believed the officer's account.

In "A Superhumanization Bias in Whites' Perceptions of Blacks," scholars relay the findings of a qualitative study that documents the "superhuman" qualities that white people attribute to Black men and women.[30] These stereotyped qualities are attributed to our minds but not our intellect, to our bodies but not our hearts. Centuries of racist rhetoric and depictions that have cast Black people as having extraordinary strength and a high tolerance for pain have shaped this flawed belief system. Theologian and seminary president Stephen G. Ray uses the term "racialized imagination" to describe a byproduct of chattel slavery that informs the American imagination through this lens and that normalizes our institutions and culture as white.[31] It is through this lens that Black people, and our culture, are depicted as "other" and outside the norm. The racialized imagination is laden with negative stereotypes about Black people and has been passed down from generation to generation. The police officer who killed Michael Brown appealed to this racist narrative to gain empathy from the jurors, and apparently, it worked. He described what he saw in his mind—an oversized human being with supernatural strength and demon eyes—and the jury apparently saw the same thing. The racialized imagination wreaks havoc on the humanity of Black people, how people *see* us, and it is not limited to males.

"You've got the wrong house!"

On February 21, 2019, Anjanette Young returned to her Chicago home after a long day's work as a licensed social worker. She went into her bedroom to change her clothes when all of the sudden she heard a loud banging, then BOOM! Nine police officers broke down her front door with a battering ram. In an interview with CBS News, Young said, "It was so traumatic to hear the thing that was hitting the door.... And it happened so fast, I didn't have time to put on clothes."[32] Police rushed in, declared they had a search warrant, and handcuffed Young as she stood *completely naked* and asking, "What is going on? There's

---

[30] Adam Waytz, Kelly Marie Hoffman, and Sophie Trawalter, "A Superhumanization Bias in Whites' Perception of Blacks" in *Social Psychological and Personality Science*. First published on October 8, 2014 doi:10.1177/1948550614553642

[31] Stephen G. Ray, Jr. "E-Racing While Black" in *Being Black, Teaching Black: Politics and Pedagogy in Religious Studies*, edited by Nancy Lynne Westfield (Nashville, TN: Abingdon Press, 2008).

[32] Dave Savini, "'You Have the Wrong Place:' Body Camera Video Shows Moments Police Handcuff Innocent, Naked Woman During Wrong Raid," CBS Chicago (CBS Chicago, December 17, 2020), https://chicago.cbslocal.com/2020/12/17/you-have-the-wrong-place-body-camera-video-shows-moments-police-handcuff-innocent-naked-woman-during-wrong-raid/

nobody else here, I live alone. I mean, what is going on here? You've got the wrong house! I live alone."

Her pleas fell on deaf ears as the officers proceeded to look for evidence that wasn't there. One of them threw a short jacket over her shoulders that still left her entire front exposed. Finally, with Young still crying and repeatedly telling them that they had the wrong house, a Black officer emerged from her bedroom with a bedspread and wrapped it around her. All of the other officers were white, and stood by with no regard for the humanity of this Black woman standing naked and crying in her own home. The person of interest did not live in that house, had never lived in that house, and was anyways wearing an electronic monitoring bracelet. Had the police officers actually done their homework, they would have known it was the wrong house.

It is difficult to imagine that if Anjanette Young were white, she would have been made to stand in her home, completely naked, while the police searched for "evidence" that did not exist. Since the founding of this country, the Black female body has had to endure the terror of being perceived as property and as expendable. From having our babies torn from our breasts on slavery auction blocks to being raped by slave masters, to "Jezebel" or "Mammy" depictions in media to politicians like Ronald Reagan using a biracial woman's story of welfare fraud to infer that Black women are "Welfare queens,"[33] the Black female body has long suffered the vulnerability of being seen through the cloak of white supremacy. Until Black bodies are seen first as human, not as property or suspects, we remain at risk of psychological and bodily harm. And the threat is not limited to Black adults.

"What did she do?"

October 26, 2015 started as an ordinary Monday at Spring Valley High School in Columbia, South Carolina. Niya Kenny sat in her algebra class and noticed there was a conversation happening with the teacher and a small group of students. The teacher asked one of the students, another Black girl, to give him her cell phone. When she did not do it, the teacher called the school resource officer into the room. The officer walked over to the student and told her to come

---

[33] Jeremy Lybarger, "The Ugly Myth of the Welfare Queen," The Nation, July 1, 2019, https://www.thenation.com/article/archive/josh-levin-the-queen-book-review/

with him. She shook her head "no," and immediately the officer put her in a headlock, flipped her over while still seated at her desk, and dragged her to the front of the classroom. The cell phone video of this harrowing incident shows how violently the officer assaulted this teen girl. Her classmate, Niya Kinney, stood up and said, "What did she do?...That's not right!" The officer came for her next, arrested her, and charged her with the crime of "disturbing school."[34]

There was nothing that this child did to warrant being physically assaulted and humiliated by this school resource officer. It should not be a crime for another student to stand up and try to stop an assault from happening. As was the case with Anjanette Young, whom officers forced to stand naked while police officers searched her apartment for "evidence," it is difficult to believe that the officer would have put a white teen girl in a headlock, flipped her over, and dragged her to the front of the classroom. But the video shows it was so. Moreover, the opportunities for student-police engagement is far greater in majority Black and Latinx schools, which is why the breaking the school-to-prison pipeline movement continues to gain traction.

"Breaking the School-to-Prison Pipeline"

Metropolitan Congregations United is a faith-based organization that empowers congregational, institutional, and community leaders to effect policy change for the common good. The organization's staff was actively involved in the Ferguson protests and has continued to tackle the issue of police violence in the St. Louis area. However, one of the hallmark campaigns that has emerged out of their Ferguson experience is breaking the school-to-prison pipeline. Rev. Dr. Dietra Wise Baker is the lead organizer of the campaign and reflected with me on some of the ways her work has changed since Ferguson:

> During Ferguson, I was a new church pastor and planter. I was also a leader in an organization called Metropolitan Congregations United, and my involvement in the movement at that time was mostly coordinating, collaborating with

---

[34] Kat Chow, "Two Years After A Violent Altercation At A S.C. High School, Has Anything Changed?," NPR (NPR, October 24, 2017), https://www.npr.org/sections/ed/2017/10/07/548510200/what-s-changed-in-south-carolina-schools-since-violent-student-arrest

clergy in the area and some lay people to be responsive to the protests that were happening and becoming a part of them. MCU, along with a lot of other folks on the ground, were coordinating safe sanctuary space and helped some of the churches to open up throughout the life cycle of the protests. A big part of my role was to build relationships with clergy and churches and folks that were in the movement that were needed resources and support—and to connect these two groups.

Since then, my church, Liberation, has closed due to [lack of] financial sustainability. We learned that sometimes new ideas for ministry are not always financially sustainable, so we went through the process of closing the church and then trying to figure out what was next.

The other part of what I was doing during Ferguson— which wasn't directly related then but it has ended up being related now—is that I had been a juvenile chaplain for fourteen years with incarcerated youth. One of the things that happened to me during all of the activism of that moment was this sort of realization that I had to begin to deal with the structures and systems, and that I couldn't just be the chaplain anymore. The impact that had on me personally, made me reflective of the system I felt like I was participating in or sometimes even being a chaplain *to* the school-to-prison pipeline system, so I had a heart-to-heart about my own role in the system. I wouldn't make myself equal with a police officer, but I was more part of the system than an advocate against it. There were things that I had seen and experienced in my role as chaplain that I knew were unjust and unfair, but I kept showing back up to work to do what the system told me I was supposed to do in that role. There was not room, at least in that chaplain role with that particular organization, to really advocate for some of the other things that I would have thought would be fair. This became very clear to me after the uprising was over. It led me onto my own journey of moving toward working in the community in a way that allows me to deal with these structures and systems straight on, particularly the ones that impacted so many of the young people that I was sitting with every day and their families.

So it's a direct line to where I am now. I'm a full-time organizer for MCU and organizing the Break the Pipeline campaign. It's a campaign to end the criminalization of Black youth in education, policing, and juvenile court systems. The movement really agitated in me the need to directly be able to confront, disrupt, and dismantle systems that, in the case of all three of these, intend to be benevolent. I think, particularly in education and even the juvenile court in its inception, ideologically, is to be treatment focused and rehabilitate young people and keep them out of prison. But we now understand these systems were collaborating and actually doing the exact opposite of their benevolent intention in terms of their impact, even though that may not be their desire or even if their historical construct in their imagination is to help. It's very clear that schools and youth policing relationships, even as it relates to what happened with Mike and definitely once they get into the hands of the supposed juvenile justice system, they're moving towards a trajectory that ends them in prison. So beginning to understand the school-to-prison pipeline as a feeder system to our mass incarceration and mass supervision systems, I wanted to be on the frontline of disrupting and dismantling these structures and systems.

Rev. Dr. Karen Anderson was the pastor of Ward Chapel AME Church in Florissant, MO, and also worked with MCU to break the school-to-prison pipeline. Rev. Anderson reflects here on her work with Break the Pipeline during her time in St. Louis:

We engage with our school districts around the St. Louis region. We've done a lot of work trying to build relationships with school districts around issues of out-of-school suspension of children, because we know that minority students are expelled at rates disproportionate to the rest of the population—usually eight times higher. So we've worked really hard with the school districts around

St. Louis trying to help them understand the difference between restorative practices for our children and these punishment models.

We've had success with our effort to end out-of-school suspension for kids in kindergarten through third grade. St. Louis Public Schools was the first school district to say "yes, we'll stop" and then we moved on to about fifteen school districts that we now have a memorandum of understanding with. They are moving toward these restorative models of discipline. They're finding ways to help keep kids in school because being out of school is not helpful to any of our children. Eventually, we hope to be able to move onto the higher grades but we're starting with the babies first.

We're also working to build relationships with the police departments, because a lot of school districts have police officers called "School Resource Officers" in the school. We want the school districts and police departments to have some memorandums of understanding that are very specific about *when* police should engage with students and *how* they engage with students. We've seen videos that have gone viral when police officers come [and] manhandle students. We're trying to make sure there are some very specific guidelines as to when the school needs to call the police. There may be some instances, but it should not be the first line of discipline.

The school resource officer that entered the Spring Valley High School classroom and attacked the young Black woman is an example of the urgent need for the kind reform that Revs. Anderson and Baker discuss.

"Why me, Mom?"

On December 26, 2020, Keyon Harrold, Jr. was staying at the Arlo Hotel in New York City with his father, Grammy Award-winning jazz musician Keyon Harrold, Sr. As they walked into the lobby, a white woman loudly accused fourteen-year-old Keyon, Jr. of stealing her cell phone. His father, who ironically is from Ferguson, began recording the incident. Throughout the video, you see the accuser making this false claim, and then physically attacking this fourteen-year-old boy.

The manager emerged and immediately sympathized with the accuser and believed her story.

The cell phone was later recovered in another location. However, young Keyon remained traumatized by the vicious accusation and assault.

In an interview on Good Morning America with Keyon Jr., Keyon Sr., Keyon Jr.'s mother Kat, and their attorney Benjamin Crump, the interviewer asked Keyon Jr. what he was thinking while this event unfolded. "I was confused...I had never seen that lady, ever." [35] It was heartbreaking to hear his mother recount how her son asked her, "Why me, Mom?" An innocent Black child going about his business was falsely accused of theft. His father exhibited extreme restraint when the accuser started attacking his son, because I am sure that he knew that if he hit her, he would be arrested—or worse. This entire family has been traumatized because of the racialized imagination of the accuser and manager who readily assumed—without a shred of evidence—that this child had stolen a cell phone. It could have ended even worse than it did. We must never forget the tragic case of sixteen-year-old Kalief Browder who was falsely accused of stealing a backpack in New York City and held in Rikers Island for three years without a trial.[36] These are not the only stories of Black children, but they are three stories too many.

Black parents are expected to have "the talk" with their sons and daughters about what to do if you are ever stopped by a police officer. Put your hands at ten and two on the steering wheel. Do not make any sudden moves. Talk slowly and clearly. Say "yes sir or no ma'am." Never, ever run.

In *Ferguson and Faith*, I discussed the Mother 2 Mother program that Christie Griffin, the executive director of the Ethics Project in St. Louis, initiated and organized. A collegium of Black mothers hosted a series of panel discussions for audiences of mostly white mothers to talk about our experiences of raising Black sons in America. In 2016, we were invited to speak at the National Civil Rights Museum

---

[35] "Activists in LA Call for Arrest of Woman Who Wrongly Accused Black Teen of Stealing Phone at NYC Hotel," ABC7 New York (WABC-TV, January 3, 2021), https://abc7ny.com/keyon-harrold-arlo-hotel-racial-profiling-black-teen-accused-of-stealing-phone/9314675/

[36] Michael Schwirtz and Michael Winerip "Kalief Browder, Held at Rikers Island for 3 Years Without Trial, Commits Suicide," The New York Times (The New York Times, June 8, 2015), https://www.nytimes.com/2015/06/09/nyregion/kalief-browder-held-at-rikers-island-for-3-years-without-trial-commits-suicide.html. Accessed September 7, 2016.

in Memphis, Tennessee, and the PBS documentary *The Talk: Race In America* captured portions of that event.[37] The pressure that Black parents have to impose upon ourselves and our children to stay safe is relentless, and the countless videos that have surfaced since Ferguson of Black people being unjustly treated—or worse—by police officers keep emerging. When will the conversation shift from Black parents talking to our children about interacting with police to elected leaders talking to police officers about how to interact with Black children? The burden should not continue to be placed on children to regulate adult behavior.

What about "Black-on-Black" crime?

One of the questions that often arises in response to police violence by people who do not believe that it is a problem is, "Well, what about 'Black-on-Black' crime?" In other words, why are you talking about the police and not about the violence in Black communities?

The follow-up question is often, "Why don't people march when Black people kill Black people, and only when the police kill a Black person?" The insinuation is that Black people do not care about community violence and are doing and saying nothing about the disproportionate homicide rates in Black communities. First, police officers are sworn to serve and protect the public. That oath is breached every time they racially profile a Black person while driving, follow them around a store without cause, or worse, kill an unarmed Black person. Policing in the United States was not established with a concern for racial justice and equity. It was quite the opposite. As citizens, we have every right to protest the long-standing inequities in the treatment of Black people by those whose tax dollars pay their salaries.

Second, there are organizations and individuals working to end gun violence. Better Family Life in St. Louis has a long-standing gun violence de-escalation program that seeks to interrupt ongoing conflict.[38] Moms Demand Action formed after the Newtown, Connecticut shootings and established chapters in every state to advocate for changes to gun laws that make us less safe.[39] Cure Violence started in Chicago in 2000 and takes a public health approach to violence reduction. The organization's

---

[37] "The Talk: Race in America," PBS (Public Broadcasting Service, February 20, 2017), https://www.pbs.org/video/talk-race-america-talk-race-america

[38] "Community Outreach," Better Family Life, October 1, 2020, https://www.betterfamilylife.org/community-outreach

[39] "Moms Demand Action," Moms Demand Action, April 20, 2020, http://www.momsdemandaction.org/

premise is that gun violence is an epidemic and must be mitigated as such, through interruption, treating those at highest risk, and changing social norms.[40] Mothers for Justice and Equality in Boston both empower mothers to challenge the normalization of violence in communities.[41] These are just a few organizations whose mission is to end gun violence.

Third, until we adequately address the conditions that create an environment conducive to gun violence, we will continue to have disproportionate rates of gun violence. Systemic racism and its corresponding effects of poverty, coupled with the proliferation of illegal guns, contribute to the astronomical homicide rates in predominately Black communities. According to the Centers for Disease Control, the primary cause of death for Black males between the ages of fifteen and forty-four is homicide. *This is the only demographic for whom this is true.* Conversely, homicide is the fourth leading cause of death for white males under nineteen, and the fifth leading cause of death for those aged nineteen to forty-four.

Gun violence in Black communities is a multifaceted problem that requires a multifaceted solution. If homicide, a preventable "illness," were the primary cause of death for *white* males or females of any age, let along under age forty-four, legislation would be passed and public health dollars would be invested in reversing that trend. However, since this is only true of Black males, any reasonable person can only conclude that systemic racism is the sole reason for there not being a widespread and comprehensive investment in ending this atrocity. Look at the legislation that was enacted to address the opioid drug crisis that largely affected white and middle-class teens and adults. The same type of sweeping effort could be applied to reducing the preventable disease of homicide among Black males by enacting legislation that would reduce the flow of guns into Black and poor neighborhoods invest in the infrastructure of economically distressed Black communities, fund public education with an equitable, not property tax-based formula and living wage training and creation. These are a few steps that would move us toward eliminating this crisis.

In 2019, the homicide rate of children in St. Louis reached a record high. The Moms group that organized the Mother's March during the Ferguson uprising gathered to hold a march in Fairground Park

---

[40] "What We Do," Cure Violence, April 21, 2020, https://cvg.org/what-we-do/

[41] "Mothers For Justice and Equality," MJE - test, March 15, 2020, https://mothersforjusticeandequality.org/

in September 2019 to raise awareness and call the city to action to curb the violence. Family members who had lost children to violence carried pictures of their offspring during the gathering, and there was a time of remembrance after the more than 250 attendees marched around the perimeter of the park.

Rev. Traci Blackmon addresses the crowd before the
Mother's March *(Photo by Stephanie Scott-Huffman)*

Rev. Karen Anderson provides guidance for
the marchers *(Photo by Stephanie Scott-Huffman)*

Desmond Francis leads the march with the
Jembe drum *(Photo by Stephanie Scott-Huffman)*

Gun Violence: A Public Health Crisis

Gun violence remains a critical problem that must be addressed with the same fervor as other pressing public health crises. In 2015, the Institute of Public Health at Washington University in St. Louis launched the Gun Violence Initiative to bring together medical professionals, scholars, and community stakeholders to investigate the data and identify solutions for gun violence reduction. In June 2020, the initiative released a five-year report that detailed their community-based preventative activities, data collection, and inquiries, and the report was submitted to the United Nations Human Rights Council in relation to gun violence and human rights.[42] This is one example of an institution's efforts to reduce gun violence and document the need

---

[42] "Gun Violence Initiative Commemorates the Past Five Years," Institute for Public Health, July 4, 2020, https://publichealth.wustl.edu/news/gun-violence-initiative-commemorates-the-past-five-years/

for the US government to invest financially in gun violence mitigation in the same way that it does other health crises such as diabetes and cancer.[43]

Gun violence devastates families and communities, and unless there are significant legislative efforts to reduce it, more guns will only mean more killing. Sadly, one of the activists I interviewed was personally impacted by the tragic effects of gun violence. DeMarco Davidson is a lead organizer for Metropolitan Congregations United (MCU) and works closely with Michael Brown, Sr.'s Chosen for Change Foundation, which was established in memory of Michael Brown, Jr. DeMarco describes some of the foundation's efforts to support fathers who have lost children to gun violence and shares his own story about how gun violence has impacted his family:

> It's been an extremely powerful experience for me since Michael Brown, Jr. was killed in Ferguson. Four years ago, I was starting seminary, and now I actually have graduated from Eden Seminary with a Master of Divinity degree. From day one of seminary, our orientation had a video that featured three alumni from Eden Seminary—Rev. Dr. Starsky Wilson, Rev. Traci Blackmon, and Rev. David Gerth.
>
> And they were sharing their views of what was going on in Ferguson at the time and how they understood it from a faith perspective. From there, I was asked to serve as the trustee of the Michael Brown Jr Memorial Fund, and... after a year of serving on that fund, we divided the money and gave it to the mother and the father of Mike Brown, Jr. Following that, I actually became the executive director of the Michael Brown Chosen for Change Foundation where I helped Michael, Sr actually organize different events, such as the past memorial days on August 9. All of these events were intended to honor the memory of Michael Brown, Jr and to bring awareness to issues that we faced.
>
> One of the best events we had was an event called "The Father's Perspective," to which we invited fathers whose

---

[43] Alison Kodjak, "What If We Treated Gun Violence Like A Public Health Crisis?," NPR (NPR, November 15, 2017), https://www.npr.org/sections/health-shots/2017/11/15/564384012/what-if-we-treated-gun-violence-like-a-public-health-crisis

children had been killed as a result of police or community violence. The event happened in 2016, and we held it at Eden Seminary, and fathers were able to just tell their stories. Some of the fathers were well-known and others weren't that well-known, but it was an amazing event. We had the father of VonDerrit Myers, Jr and Cary Ball, both of who[m] were from St. Louis. We also had the father of Jordan Davis who was killed in Jacksonville after being confronted by a man at a gas station telling him to turn his music down, and fathers like Brother Bolden, who is the father of Jamyla Bolden. A stray bullet that hit her house killed nine-year-old Jamyla in 2015. It was a mixture of fathers, and they just told their stories.

One of the reasons I was so honored to host that event is because, unfortunately, I lost my father. He was killed in his house by a nineteen-year-old in 2015. On the night of my dad's death, my brother and I decided to go to a local restaurant to wait while the police did their work. It was very late, probably two or three in the morning, and out of nowhere, Mike Brown, Sr walks in. He asked me what I was doing, and I asked him, "What are you doing here?"

I told him what happened to my dad, and he started crying. I hadn't even shed any tears yet for my dad, but Mike Brown, Sr was crying for me. And ever since then, we've just had a certain bond with each other, and we've shed tears for each other many times since then. So it was an honor for me to be able to bring these fathers together so they could share their stories and support each other. And they were free to say whatever they wanted. One of the fathers asked me, "What should or shouldn't I say?" And I told him that he could say whatever he wanted. He was surprised because they've had other events where the organizers ask them to keep it at a certain level and not really show all of their experiences and all of their hurt.

February 14, 2018 is the date the seventeen students and adults were killed at Marjory Stoneman Douglas High School in Parkland, Florida. Marjory Stoneman Douglas (1890–1998) was a suffragette, writer, journalist, and environmental activist who worked tirelessly to conserve the Florida Everglades. One of her famous quotes—"Be a nuisance when it counts. Do your part to inform and stimulate the public to join your action. Be depressed, discouraged & disappointed at failure & the disheartening effects of ignorance, greed, corruption & bad politics—but never give up"—was put on a sign outside of the high school after the massacre.[44] A group of students responded and formed March For Our Lives advocacy group for gun violence prevention. With more than one hundred chapters across the country, they are the largest youth-led effort to reduce gun violence through public policy and safe practices in the United States.[45] DeMarco describes some of the leaders from March For Our Lives visiting with Ferguson activists in June 2018:

Meeting with March For Our Lives activists in
June 2018 *(Photo courtesy of DeMarco Davidson)*

One Father's Day, I knew it was going to be a tough day for Mike Brown, Sr, and somehow he was connected with the students from Parkland. And we were able to welcome some of the students. Mike's wife catered and provided food for

[44] AJ Willingham, "In the Wave of Walkouts, a Quote from Marjory Stoneman Douglas Becomes a Rallying Cry," CNN (Cable News Network, March 14, 2018), https://www.cnn.com/2018/03/14/us/marjory-stoneman-douglas-quote-walkout-trnd/index.html

[45] "March For Our Lives," March For Our Lives, June 15, 2019, https://marchforourlives.com/

the students while they were here. I shared with them that we are now living in a time where it seems like almost every day is now a day of infamy for a horrible, terrible reason. We remember August 9, 2014 because of Michael Brown, Jr. We're going to remember February 14, 2018 because of the massacre in Parkland. I even remember where I was. I was at the Samuel DeWitt Proctor Conference when I heard about the Parkland school shooting. I can't believe that this keeps happening. The students [visiting] from Parkland were fourteen or thirteen when Mike Brown was killed, and some of them talked about how they were able to find their voice by seeing other young people in Ferguson. Even in the midst of tragedy, the youth and young people on the streets in Ferguson helped people find their voice or inspired them to maintain it.

SENSORY WORK

Words affect all of our senses. They are carriers of more than just thoughts or ideas: they transmit energy that influence how we feel, think, dream, and imagine. Words, and the meanings we derive from them, are powerful beyond measure.

I invite you to consider a time when the words you heard (or spoke) played into the racialized imagination:

- Where were you?
- Who said them?
- What was the speaker trying to achieve by saying them?
- How did they make your feel?
- How did you respond?

Sometimes these words come from people holding press conferences and news stories but other times they are spoken in our presence.

I encourage you to consider how you might respond if you are present as derogatory words or coded racist sentiments are spoken about Black people:

- Will you remain silent?
- What might you say?
- How will you determine whether to remain silent or speak?

* * *

Death and life are in the power of the tongue, and those who love it will eat its fruits. —Proverbs 18:21 (NRSV)

CHAPTER 4

....

Bitter Dregs of Discomfort

Seventeen years ago I lost my sense of taste. I was attending a conference in New Orleans, and after dinner one evening, I started to feel lightheaded. Not thinking much of it (even though I had only had water to drink), I returned to my hotel room and decided to lie down. However, I could barely walk straight by then, so I decided to go to the emergency room. At this point, it felt like the entire hospital was spinning and through slurred words, I had to try and explain to the attending nurse that I was not intoxicated but was seriously ill. She gave me a side-eye, wheeled me into the back, and even after bloodwork was taken, could not figure out what was wrong. "Maybe it was something you ate?" the doctor said.

By the time I returned home to Ohio and soon afterward moved to St. Louis, the dizziness had become intermittent, but my sense of taste was completely gone. I had to orient my mind and body to a world without the capacity to savor the flavor of my favorite ice cream, know if I had too much salt on my food, or tell the difference between Schnuck's or Straub's rotisserie chicken.

Everything I ate and drank tasted the same, which was no identifiable flavor at all. One of the challenges with everything tasting the same is that you may be tempted to start believing that everything *is* the same, when in reality there are distinct differences between salmon and a Snickers bar. Fortunately for me, my taste returned three years later without any fanfare or warning. It just showed up one afternoon as I was eating a turkey sandwich, for which I am eternally grateful.

What does it mean to awaken your sense of taste in the work of racial justice? To remain taste-less in the context of racial justice is to believe that everyone's experience is basically the same. It's the "I don't see color" or "All Lives Matter" stances. A position of white privilege permits people to believe that if Black people do not have the same privileges, then it's their own fault because racism doesn't exist. Awakening your taste in the pursuit of racial justice requires that you take seriously the testimonies or facts that are being served to you. From a position of racial privilege, they will likely taste bitter and make you feel unpleasant. However, if we are to understand the truth about Black people's experiences and seek to forge an equitable way forward, we must be willing to taste the bitter dregs of discomfort. Dismantling racism and white supremacy is not your feel-good type of work. It is arduous, painful, and for some, quite alienating. But we cannot progress without entering the difficult space of listening, sharing, and being open to transformation.

Sacred Conversations about Race

Metropolitan Congregations United (MCU), an interfaith consortium of religious congregations, hosted a series of Sacred Conversations on Race after the Ferguson uprising. Rev. David Gerth, the executive director, has been actively involved in organizing these efforts and engaged in many of the protests. He describes this initiative and the responses the MCU received in the St. Louis area:

I think that there are lots of congregations and people of faith who are really interested in seeing policies changed and power shifted. But even more than that, I think people want to talk about what race means. And that doesn't necessarily mean that they want to go and work on it, but there's an interest and a fascination that is sometimes really positive and they show up and say, "I've been to a conversation that was good," and they feel like they've done something. But what we hope they would say is "Well, that was interesting. That was challenging. Now I have to figure out what I'm going to do." That's the outcome we're looking for from a conversation. And church folks often have trouble with that.

I find we have trouble if we're going to change the Sunday School curriculum or time of worship or the hymnal we're going to use or how we respond to structural racism. We'd rather think about it a little longer than make a decision and move forward. And I think with race, it's even harder for us to actually move. We're so afraid of something blowing up. I also think, on the other hand, that there are people who really have no interest in talking about it at all ever again. Some people said in the week after Michael Brown was killed, "When are we going to get back to normal?" Well, that hasn't ended. Some people are still hoping that someday we'll get back to "normal."

There are sociologists and church theorists that will tell you that a congregation that can disagree about hard topics like what salvation is or what you think about the president are congregations that are much more likely to grow and thrive than ones that avoid any kind of controversy. But most of us don't really believe that. Those of us who have any type of leadership responsibility need to help each other have whatever the next risky, challenging conversation is so that we get a little better at having the next even harder one.

When we were in the Sacred Conversations on Race program in the winter of 2015, it ultimately helped us build our Break the Pipeline campaign. In those days, we were still feeling tremendous urgency that there should be actual, noticeable shifts in policy, practices, and procedures all up and down the line. Not just with police and the courts but in our schools and our churches. All of us needed to be shifting the way that we interacted with each other and start pressing against structural racism in our communities. And so we just pushed, and people came to those conversations expecting to be a little uncomfortable, and not everybody stuck around, but we weren't really that worried. We felt like it was our job to help people enter into that discomfort.

Rev. Dr. Dietra Wise Baker also worked with this effort and reflects on the challenge of doing the work of having difficult conversations, as well as some of the positive changes in St. Louis:

For Metropolitan Congregations United (MCU), we did this big effort for Sacred Conversations on Race, and we had a huge response of about five hundred people at one time, and then were involved in a series of conversations on race. In St. Louis overall, there has been a huge uptick in conversations about race, racism, and white privilege. Not so much of white supremacy, but it's getting there. I think white supremacy brings in a sort of historical conversation about events and actions of people in power against another group, and those are harder conversations to have. It's seems very hard for white folks to have that factual and historical conversation about race. [Instead,] they often want to have...conversations about Black experiences and tend to be voyeuristic about what it feels like to be Black instead of [reflecting personally on] the historical legacy of white people in this country and beyond. It's a long trail of white supremacy and domination in this land and in others.

A very small percentage of people are controlling the wealth in this country, and there has been a historical narrative to pit non-rich white people against Black people by saying that the problems you're experiencing in your economic and social life are because of the gains that people of color are experiencing...when the truth is that one percent of the people have 63 percent of the wealth, and we're just fighting for the scraps here at the bottom.

But one of the things I see when I look at the organizing world and the demographic graphs, they have 63 percent of the money but we have 99 percent of the people. And what can happen if we build a coalition of organized people? We hands-down have the advantage on the people side, so if we can begin to break down these narratives and tell the truth about what's happening in our economy, what's happening in our democracy, [then] we can build a pretty awesome collaborative. I feel like people are starting to wake up, they're getting a little less sleepy. When you put the raw data in front of folks, particularly around economics, people are starting to wake up.

Just because you know about a justice issue doesn't mean that you do anything about it. Just because you go to a conference or a panel discussion doesn't mean something will change. Although I'm grateful for Sacred Conversations on Race, we called ours Sacred Conversations on Race *plus action*. After the conference ends and you finish talking, what are you actually going to do? What are you going to push on, press on, pull on, dismantle, disrupt within an actual system? What are you going to win? How are we going to know we won? What's going to change or did we just talk and educate ourselves about all the problems but we haven't taken any steps to begin to reimagine and implement a solution? So that's what I've been thinking about these days. I've been thinking about organizing and what it means for people who have been impacted by these issues to be at the center of them and build enough power to drive the kind of community they want to see. I've been thinking about what it means to move from charity to doing justice where, in everything we do, we're dismantling systems that have been death-dealing to people of color and to people who are marginalized and oppressed.

Rev. Rebecca Ragland is the pastor of St. Paul's Episcopal Church, Carondolet, in St. Louis. During the Ferguson uprising, she led the Episcopal Service Corp intern ministry and several of its members in the activist efforts. She reflects on some of the challenges of pastoring people with different socio-political perspectives:

There was one person in particular who knew that I was involved in the Ferguson uprising but held a different perspective than I did. We talked, and I began to feel like we could have a rapport in spite of these differences. But it also then created this crisis, and I've subsequently felt like I have this crisis in ministry quite a bit which is: where do I hold people accountable just the way I hold systems accountable? And how do I do that as a pastor when I don't agree with their position or their behavior? That whole issue of the interpersonal relationships across political differences if you want to call it that or social differences or sort of loyalties even, to me, that is an ongoing discernment that I would like to feel like I had more resources to kind of help me think those issues out, because the sweet thing about protesting is that there is a line. And, if you're on this side, it's this, and if you're on the opposite side, it's the opposite. But so much of our lives, especially as a pastor, there is so much nuance and so much discernment about how to approach issue and morality. So I think Ferguson has helped me to find my inner courage and my voice for conviction, and also helped me to see that what fundamentally people are looking for is to be heard and to be walked with, and that this person that I had definitely perceived as someone I could never hear from or walk with, now I'm walking with. And that's not as easy as yelling across the way at someone. But somehow, it's got to be both. Right? There has to be a courage to do the protesting, but there also has to be the courage to have those difficult conversations in your community.

This congregation that I'm in right now is definitely purple. I think there's more blue than red, but there is certainly some red. And so that mix of purple, to me, we are trying to figure out how to have those conversations. I've been thinking about this, particular[ly] this idea of the red and the blue if you think about just our political parties, and the mix of that is purple, and that, liturgically, our colors for Lent and Advent, for these penitential seasons, are purple. And thinking about how to get us mixed. I don't have enough experience yet to say if—to say I have tried this and it's really true. I've begun conversations, and it seems to be true that, if you just ask questions and you create a safe space for them, that people ... want to engage in that and they're hungry to find ways across those differences, especially now when our whole cultural conversation is so strident. I think there's really a longing among people. So I say: do it. Better to do it and name these things than to avoid it and continue with the status quo, which is simply allowing the decay of our society and the common good.

Rev. Ragland continues to reflect on one of her experiences of having a challenging conversation and the opportunity it presented for greater understanding that was not realized:

My experience right after Ferguson, I was asked to talk in different churches that were mostly Lutheran, Evangelical Lutheran, or Episcopal churches. And my sense is that the churches are just like the rest of the culture in terms of the binary commitments. Some just seem that they can't get past saying "Well, police officers are just trying to do their jobs."

I recently went to a neighborhood association meeting in the area where my church is located. A police officer was the guest speaker for the one-hour meeting, and he easily talked for forty-five minutes. He was very charming and engaging, and I found myself laughing at some of his jokes when he talked about getting in trouble because he had cursed at this guy and then kicked his SUV because he was driving a four-wheeler on a road, and he got in trouble. And it was kind of funny the way he was describing it, but …it definitely gave me this feeling inside like that second consciousness of where is the accountability? Where do I hold them accountable? For instance, he was saying crime rates had gone down significantly in our area, and he credited this to increased policing.

Well, I would want to say there are a lot of reasons why the crime rate has gone down in that area. You look at the economy. People are getting jobs significantly more. You look at the churches. We have now at least three churches that are providing meals on a fairly regular basis. So I'm sitting there as the only clergyperson in the neighborhood meeting, nodding and laughing, and he's saying things that… I mean it's my obligation to raise my hand and say, "You know, I appreciate what the police do, but I also want to point out there are a lot of reasons why the crime rate has gone down." Wouldn't that have been an appropriate thing to do? Did I do it? No. And so, how to stay woke because I wasn't woke at that neighborhood meeting. So how to do that is important because those situations are missed opportunities.

Rev. Dr. Deborah Krause is the president of Eden Seminary in St. Louis and was actively involved in the Ferguson uprising. During that time, she served as dean of Eden Seminary and worked to bridge the gaps between the streets, church, and theological education. She reflects on the importance of theological education preparing students to make these kinds of connections:

As a theological educator, I think about how we prepare our students to help extend their congregations' connections into the community. It's not that all of our students or alumni are going to be organizers. However, they need to be thinking about networking that way and connecting their congregations to other organizations, be they other religious or nonreligious communities, to collaborate and make change because these systems are so big. A single church usually isn't going to be able to do much. We aren't the spaces in which the light is first coming on about this so we need to move ourselves into those spaces. We need to be willing to get up out of this place and realize that God is speaking and moving and calling us to hear others.

And I think that's the step that the churches in St. Louis, that are vitally growing after Ferguson and finding a lane, are doing it more in this sort of networked way than "Huh, let's hunker down here and decide how we're going to fix this." No, they are asking "Where in our community are there the leaders and the people that have the wisdom about this? How can we move into their spaces and learn from them?" They're offering, "If we were to collaborate with you, these are the commitments and insight, beliefs and resources we have to bring. What of that would be of help to you?"

As I think the faith communities that are thinking that way, I think of Josh Privitt at St. Peters in Ferguson. The day after Michael Brown was executed and we were in the parking lot of the police department, I remember looking out, seeing Josh Privitt. His eyes were as big as saucers. He had just started at St. Peters in Ferguson, and Josh not only was putting himself out there going to protest, but he was also identifying ways in which to connect his community to leaders and activists and workers for justice in Ferguson that could broaden his congregation's understanding of its belonging to the larger community.

I believe he wanted them to see their vocation as more integrally related to Black kids in Ferguson who were getting harassed by the police. I just don't think that would have happened if Josh hadn't been there and involved because it does take a leader to compel a congregation to move that way. It doesn't have to be an ordained leader, but I think in this case, Josh was key. And I think the church is in a position to have a much more clear answer to its "why." And, in some way, I think that Ferguson created an opportunity. It almost feels like a sacrilege to say that it created an opportunity. But the uprising created an opportunity, I think, for congregations to wake up to their why, and a couple of them have.

Rev. Josh Privitt is the Eden Seminary graduate that President Krause describes above. Josh is the associate pastor at St. Peter's United Church of Christ in Ferguson. Below he shares his experience of helping a predominately white congregation enter into the challenging work of difficult conversations about race, and living into their "why":

I started at St. Peter's a week and a day before Mike Brown was killed and was thrown right into ministry. As I came into that role, it became very clear very quickly that, at least for a good while, my community ministry role was going to be just standing and being with folks who were raising their voices and rightfully saying that Ferguson's got a racism problem. My role, especially as a white male pastor, was not to try and be one of those on the frontlines but to support the ones who were and who were saying the things that needed to be said.

Our congregation makeup is about half of folks who actually live outside of Ferguson and about half who either live in Ferguson or one of the other close-by municipalities. We had responses ranging from folks who were coming on Sunday mornings to try to escape the chaos that was going on around them. We had folks who were coming in and wanting to jump right in with the protests and raise their voices and do the social justice advocacy that was happening. And we had folks in between who were still sort of deciding what was going on and trying to discern exactly what the conversation was about when folks were talking about race and racism. They couldn't see what the issues were at the time—sort of a classic white privilege standpoint, just not even able to understand what the issue was.

Before I came, some pastors before me had started the conversation of what does it look like to be a church in a formerly white neighborhood that has now transitioned into a mostly nonwhite neighborhood? And what does it look like for us as a church, that is probably 75 percent white, to do ministry in a community that doesn't look like us? What came out was that we can no longer be the "traditional family neighborhood church," that we needed to do the work of community building and provide support beyond our walls. That's the reason my position was developed.

There have been numerous situations where we've had conversations that have just popped up around race and racism in terms of the meaning of white privilege and why folks are protesting. I think the groundwork hasn't been laid to say this is not just going to be like a white people bashing kind of session, but this is actually a deep conversational about what it looks like to be a bigger, wider, and more inclusive community. What's worked well in our setting have been those much more informal, smaller conversations that are starting to unpack questions like "Am I privileged as a white person?" and "Is there racism inherent in the system?"

For this congregation, starting with those smaller conversations can often be the jumping off point to the bigger conversations with larger groups of people having even tougher and deeper questions. And I've just learned to play the long game and the patience game, even though for me, I'm like "Yeah, let's talk about this." But sometimes it takes a little bit more work to get there—which can be frustrating beyond all reason, but that's kind of the long wick of history in some ways. For centuries, we have been unwilling to acknowledge racism and overcoming that is long work.

I remember one particular sermon that I gave [in which] I knew I was going to talk about my own learning of white privilege and inner racism. We had our liturgy focus on healing and wholeness so that we were trying to provide space where people could rejuvenate and at the same time push themselves. When I talked about race and racism, I talked in the first person. I wasn't trying to tell people what to think, but instead [was] saying, "Here is my experience, and here's where I came from, and here's how I learned about it." The Sunday I did this my parents were in the audience, and I was talking about being raised in a way that tried to treat everyone—despite skin color, despite height difference, despite belief difference—as beloved children of God. But on the one hand, this is what was being told to me, and on the other hand when we would go to big cities and see a lot of nonwhite folks, my mom would tell my dad to put his billfold in the front pocket. So these mixed messages were coming through. I always talked from firsthand experience more than anything and used that as a jumping off place to say, "And here's how I know that we've still got a long way to go.

Protest march through the Butler Tarkington neighborhood in Indianapolis after the killing of George Floyd on June 8, 2020. Participants gathered at Common Ground Christian Church and marched through the upper-middle-class neighborhood and concluded at the Martin Luther King Center. *(Photo by Carrie Smith-Coons)*

Here's how I know that the protestors have something to say to us." As a newer pastor in the setting, I think it was incredibly helpful for folks to know a little bit more about me personally. When I was sharing that, it allowed them to see that I was a human being and connect with me in a way they couldn't if I was just talking generally and "objectively." It was scary, but it was also really good to be able to share that vulnerable place, and hopefully, it opened up space for others to do the same.

Rev. Jeff Krajewski, pastor of Common Ground Church in Indianapolis, speaks to the protestors at the conclusion of the Butler Tarkington march. *(Photo by Carrie Smith-Coons)*

Conversations about race and racism do not have to be limited to individual conversations. Rev. Julie Taylor describes how these issues were addressed within the Unitarian Universalist (UU) denomination and not merely within a few congregations:

In early 2017, we had a big explosion within the (UU) denomination around white supremacy. The long and short of it was there was a national staff position as a regional leader for one of our regions. It was announced that a white male, who was not even from the region, got this position. Around this time, the Religious Professionals of Color were meeting and it came out that a Latinx woman who lives in that region was also up for that job and did not get it. A group of us got together and wrote a letter to the president of our denomination, signed it, and put it on the ministers' Facebook group and ended up with around 120 signatures. After a lot of back and forth within a few months, there were three top-level resignations. It became a huge issue in the denomination.

So within a few weeks there were three religious educators [who] put together curriculum and called for a denomination-wide white supremacy teach-in for congregations. More than seven hundred out of roughly one thousand congregations participated in a white supremacy teach-in with about a three-week notice. They put together the curriculum and basically said, "Over the course of two Sundays, we want to see as many congregations as possible sign up and commit to doing some kind of teach-in. Whatever you have planned for the pulpit, get rid of it." And more than seven hundred congregations did. It happened differently for everyone. For some, lay leaders led it as a religious education [class] after church. For others, it was integrated into the entire service. The process varied and was able to be done organically within the congregation. But more than two-thirds of our congregations did that within the short time frame, which is kind of remarkable.

There was huge pushback around what the words "white supremacy" mean, and that continues to be the case. Some people say, "If we're going to talk about white supremacy as UUs, what does that make the KKK folks or the tiki torch people?" So we've had to work at helping people understand the difference between white supremacists and white supremacy—and racism more generally. Some found it easier to push back on the [term] white supremacist because they can point to the tiki torch bearers and say, "I'm not doing that." But back in 2015 and 2016 when a lot of congregations had Black Lives Manner banners, it was often met with "Yeah, but all lives matter"—which is a dismissal of the claim by Black people that their lives [currently] do not matter in the same way as white lives. There were a lot of Black Lives Matter banners that were torn down or stolen during this time.

Black Lives Matter banners were not only vandalized and stolen back in 2015; it has continued to this day. The protests that erupted across the country after the killing of George Floyd in Minneapolis sparked a public renewal of the Black Lives Matter mantra, and, unfortunately, its corresponding "All Lives Matter" (or worse) backlash. I was surprised—actually shocked—to see Black Lives Matter signs emerge in my own sparsely diverse neighborhood. It started with one or two, then over the course of the summer they continued to pop up like tulips in springtime. My impulse was to start knocking on doors and inquiring about the residents' decision to make this public statement in our neighborhood, but I resisted and drew my own conclusions. Notices were sent out on one of our neighborhood apps that signs had been stolen but many remain.

Churches have also continued to put Black Lives Matter signs and hang banners outside of their buildings. One of the most visible church banners in the Indianapolis community was hung on the St. Paul's Episcopal Church, a predominately white and affluent church that is nestled along one of the busiest thoroughfares between the Indianapolis northern suburbs and downtown. The rector, Rev. John Denson, was interviewed by a local reporter, Katiera Winfrey, about the church's decision to make such a decisively clear statement. Rev. Denson noted that they could have responded to previous killings, but they were not going to sit this one out. The leadership decided to respond to Floyd's killing as plainly as possible.

"We thought about what signs we could put up. So we wanted to put just Black Lives Matter, because we wanted to make it clear where we stand as a community of faith, and we don't want to shrink back and just make statements. The other thing is that the sign in and of itself is not sufficient. It's fine to put up a sign, but the question is, 'How does that call us as a people to live into the gospel?'"[46]

Yes, the church received phone calls from members and neighbors expressing dismay and asking why they didn't hang an "All Lives Matter" sign, but that did not deter them or make them change

---

[46] Katiera Winfrey, "'We Stand Together': Rev. John Denson, St. Paul's Episcopal Church - WISH-TV: Indianapolis News: Indiana Weather: Indiana Traffic," WISH, July 29, 2020, https://www.wishtv.com/community/westandtogether/we-stand-together-rev-john-denson-st-pauls-episcopal-church.

course. "Our response was well, yes, all lives matter. Of course all lives matter, but we live in a time in society in which that's not lived out systemically. In the structures and systems in which we live, all lives are not valued. And so, sometimes you have to name the specific lives that are not being valued in order to claim that they are [of value]."[47]

St. Paul Episcopal Church in Indianapolis, July 2020
(Photo by Leah Gunning Francis)

The "How does that call us as a people to live into the gospel?" question related to racial justice is one on which this church continues to work. Rev. Denson noted several of the ways the church has worked to build relationships with organizations like the Martin Luther King Center and to provide support to one of the local public schools. In response to the deaths of Floyd and Dreasjon Reed, a young Black man killed by an Indianapolis police officer during a car-turned-foot chase on May 6, 2020, Rev. Patrick Burke, parish missioner at St. Paul's, co-led an ecumenical response team along with Alexis Tardy, Zionsville Christian Church's Faith Formation Director (and Eden Seminary

---

[47] Ibid

alumnus), Rev. Chana Tetzlaff, associate rector of St. Christopher's Episcopal Church, and Rev. Mary Dicken, pastor of Mission and Discipleship at Meridian Street United Methodist Church.

The response movement was called F.A.S.T. (Faith Aid Support Team), and its mission was to provide physical and spiritual support for the protestors against racial injustice. The team invited clergy from around the area to join in this effort as a way to stand in solidarity in a tangible way. Those who did not feel comfortable being a physical presence/participant at the protests were invited to contact local elected officials to support the demands of groups such as Indy10 Black Lives Matter, Indiana Racial Justice Alliance, or Faith in Indiana.

This kind of clergy and church activism and advocacy was also encouraged by the diocesan bishop, The Right Rev. Jennifer Baskerville-Burrows. During a Zoom meeting with other Episcopal bishops in June 2020, Bishop Baskerville-Burrows reflected on her own experiences of racism and issued a clarion call to her beloved church to engage actively in the work of racial justice:

> So here is the challenge for the Episcopal Church: We need to stop being afraid of committing to the work of dismantling systemic racism and white supremacy. We need to learn and understand how it operates inside the Episcopal Church and in the world. As a predominately white institution that is rooted in the American experiment, we must be unequivocal and clear. When I go to the webpage of Ben & Jerry's Ice Cream, it is clear that they are about selling ice cream and dismantling white supremacy. I want our church to be that clear. Our being afraid of making white people upset makes us complicit in keeping white supremacy in place. We must not be afraid of giving our time and financial resources to the groups who are doing this work on the ground.[48]

---

[48] Jennifer Baskerville-Burrows, "From Bishop Jennifer: A Reflection of Personal Experience, Hope and Challenge for the Church on Dismantling White Supremacy and Racism," Episcopal Diocese of Indianapolis, July 7, 2020, https://indydio.org/from-bishop-jennifer-a-reflection-of-personal-experience-hope-and-challenge-for-the-church-on-dismantling-white-supremacy-and-racism/

Even if you are not a member of an Episcopal congregation, I strongly encourage you to read Bishop Baskerville-Burrows entire statement (in English or Spanish) and consider its implications for your own experience and context. The work of dismantling racism and white supremacy is a critical way in our time to "live into the gospel," for the forces working to maintain this dehumanizing status quo are working overtime.

A Black Lives Matter banner hangs outside of the Friendship-West Baptist Church in Dallas, Texas. *(Photo courtesy of Friendship-West Baptist Church)*

The targeting of churches with Black Lives Matter signs has taken many troubling forms. On August 2, 2020, a "Back the Blue" biker cruise of motorcycles and big wheeled trucks carrying Confederate and US flags, was making a hundred-mile ride through Texas in an alleged show of support for police after the killing of George Floyd. They descended *en masse* and uninvited on the parking lot of Friendship-West Baptist Church, a tactic that the pastor, Rev. Dr. Freddy Haynes, considered to be one of intimidation:

> We did not approve them. For this kind of intimidation to take place where they come to our community and choose a church that has that sign up on it, Black Lives Matter, it was an act of intimidation. As far as I am concerned, it is almost as if they were trying to declare war on us. They just

need to know that you will not come to Oak Cliff, you will not come to Friendship-West and act like Black lives don't matter, because they do.[49]

Protestors calling for justice in Dallas, Texas, for Botham Jean and O'Shae Terry who were killed by police in 2018. Protestors gathered at Friendship-West Baptist Church and marched to the Dallas Stadium, where the Cowboys were playing. The march was led by pastor of Friendship-West Rev. Dr. Freddy Haynes and attorney Lee Merritt, Rev. Michael Waters, and Imam Omar Suleiman. *(Photo courtesy of Friendship-West Baptist Church)*

Dr. Haynes and Friendship-West Baptist Church are well-known for engaging in and leading the movement for racial justice in the Dallas area. The picture below is from a 2018 protest.

On the night of December 12, 2020, members of the white supremacist hate group Proud Boys descended on Washington, DC. This is the same group that President Trump called by name during the September presidential debate and told to them "stand back and stand by" in response to the protests against police violence. It is worth noting that the alleged leader of the Proud Boys is of Cuban descent and worth remembering too that defenders of white supremacy come in many colors. This is one of the reasons why it is never sufficient merely

[49] Erin Jones, "Frustration Grows After Oak Cliff Church Says 'Back The Blue' Cruise Showed Up To Parking Lot Uninvited," CBS Dallas / Fort Worth (CBS Dallas / Fort Worth, August 2, 2020), https://dfw.cbslocal.com/2020/08/02/frustration-grows-oak-cliff-church-says-back-the-blue-cruise-showed-up-uninvited/

to elect/hire/appoint a "person of color" as an indicator of equality and racial justice. Movement toward equity and racial justice does not occur without a commitment and investment by the church, company, organization, or school to dismantle the system of racial injustice that perpetuates the status quo.

When the Proud Boys and company came to Washington, DC in support of the president's "Stop the Steal" movement, they targeted at least three churches' Black Lives Matter signs: Metropolitan AME Church, Asbury United Methodist Church, and Luther Place Memorial Church. Video footage blazed across social media of signs being torn down and one being drenched in lighter fluid and burned. Onlookers cheered in a way reminiscent of lynching, cross burning, home bombings, and neighborhood night raids. Each of the pastors spoke out against this act of terror. Rev. William Lamar, pastor of Metropolitan AME, wrote an op-ed for *The Washington Post*:

> A sign came down on Saturday. The Black Lives Matter banner in front of Metropolitan African Methodist Episcopal Church, where I am privileged to serve as pastor, was removed and destroyed on Saturday evening. I am deeply disturbed by this incident (one of several incidents targeting houses of worship), but I am more disturbed by the continued mythology of imperial America. This mythology supports those who commit violence against human beings for political ends, deny citizens their right to vote, denigrate sacred spaces, and claim as their own whatever they survey.
>
> It mattered not that the land was ours. It mattered not that the sign was ours. The mythology that motivated the perpetrators on Saturday night was the underbelly of the American narrative—that White men can employ violence to take what they want and do what they want and call that criminality justice, freedom, and liberty.[50]

Rev. Lamar issues a clarion call for our country that is steeped in white supremacy and capitalism, or perhaps what Dr. James Lawson

[50] William H. Lamar, "Opinion: My Church Will Replace Our Black Lives Matter Sign. Will America Replace Its Racist Myth?," The Washington Post (WP Company, December 21, 2020), https://www.washingtonpost.com/opinions/2020/12/15/dc-metropolitan-ame-church-vandalized-blm-sign

calls "plantation capitalism," to abandon its god of white supremacy and join the work of God in forging a new way forward that honors the humanity and thriving of all. We should not disconnect the desecration of the churches Black Lives Matter signs from the devastating attack at Emanuel AME Church in Charleston, South Carolina. This historic Black church, affectionately known as Mother Emanuel, was hosting its weekly Bible study when a stranger joined in on June 17, 2015. The church members did as the Bible implores us to do and welcomed the stranger, a young white man named Dylann Roof, who sat through the entire Bible study with them. As they prepared to have a departing prayer, instead of holding hands, Roof held out his semi-automatic weapon and fired at will. He killed nine people and traumatized many others by this heinous act of racial terror:

> *Cynthia Graham Hurd, 54*
>
> *Susie J. Jackson, 87*
>
> *Ethel Lance, 70*
>
> *DePayne Middleton-Doctor, 49*
>
> *Rev. Clementa C. Pinckney, 41*
>
> *Tywanza Kibwe Diop Sanders, 26*
>
> *Daniel Lee Simmons Sr., 74*
>
> *Sharonda Coleman-Singleton, 45*
>
> *Myra Singleton Quarles Thompson, 59*

Rev. Dr. Jacque Foster, pastor of Compton Heights Christian Church in St. Louis, challenges us to consider the influences that nurture and encourage the kind of racial terror that occurred at Mother Emanuel AME Church:

> So many times we've thought, "Well, when this generation dies things are going to get better." Seeing the acts in Charlottesville by young adults with tiki torches says to us that this is not something that is generational and is going to go away. This is something that is nurtured and taught

to children. The hard question is, "What are we doing, as a society, that nurtures and continues this hatred?" It's easy for me to want to pass on that and say "Well, their parents are teaching them this." But maybe it's not that simple. What are we doing, as a society, to grow, if you will, our own white supremacists?

When I looked at the picture in the paper of the young man who had just been convicted and sentenced for the murders at Emmanuel Church in Charleston I said, "This is a young man. What created this in him?" This is what makes it even more important for us as the church to teach and be clear about what we are teaching, not just in theory but to build relationships between people.

Christian Nationalism and White Supremacy

One of the narratives that has long been perpetuated by leaders in this country is that the United States is a Christian nation, when the truth is that it is a country of many faith traditions and cultures. I have never heard a leader make the Christian nation claim then follow it up with concrete examples of how our country's laws and social practices follow in the way of Christ's mandates of loving our neighbors, caring for the poor, or treating others the way we would want to be treated. Instead, the conflation of Christianity and nationality has done more to buttress the position of white supremacy than creating an egalitarian society. The Poor People's Campaign: A National Call for Moral Revival, a cross-racial, multi-faith movement that started during the Civil Rights era, has been reignited by Rev. Dr. William Barber and Rev. Dr. Liz Theoharis. This initiative calls attention to the racial, structural, economic, educational, and healthcare inequalities and rejects the privileging of a Christian nationalist agenda that does little beyond putting a "Christian" stamp of approval on the status quo of inequity in our country.[51] The tethering of Christianity, nationalism, and white supremacy is not a new concept; however, the time has come for followers of Christ to make a choice. For too many individual Christians and congregations, there is no separation from the cross of Christ and the US flag—in a country that prides itself on the faux separation of church and state.

---

[51] "Poor People's Campaign," Poor People's Campaign, October 3, 2020, https://www.poorpeoplescampaign.org/

The time has come to remove the United States flags from our sanctuaries. There is no sound theological justification for having them as permanent fixtures in our sacred spaces of worship. If we are serious about moving toward being a country that is just and equitable for all, we must take seriously the way that the flag and its symbolic meaning has been weaponized against Black and/or immigrant people, and it should not be a point of worship in our sanctuaries. The "Make America Great Again (MAGA)" supporters posture themselves as the "real Americans," and anyone that doesn't believe as they do can go back to where they came from.[52]

One of the most brazen and offensive conflations of Christianity, nationalism, and white supremacy occurred during protests that emerged after George Floyd was killed.

Protests erupted in cities, towns, and hamlets across the country after video emerged of a Minneapolis police officer kneeling on the neck of George Floyd for 8 minutes and 46 seconds until he lay lifeless on the street. The world witnessed Floyd begging for help and saying he couldn't breathe. His cries were joined by some of the bystanders imploring the officer to stop, but the pleas were ignored. Near the end of his life, Floyd called for his deceased mother, Larcenia Floyd. "Momma! Momma, I'm through," were some of his last words before he took his final breath.

The casual callousness of the officer's actions. Other officers standing around and doing nothing to stop the murder. The cries of the crowd. The video of Floyd's murder being filmed by a seventeen-year-old Black girl: This Memorial Day murder was a tipping point that resulted in thousands taking to the streets across the United States for weeks and saying "Enough!" Enough of the state-sanctioned killing of unarmed Black people.

A Minneapolis police precinct was set ablaze during the third night of protests as demands were made for all of the officers involved to be arrested. By this time, the president was threatening to deploy the National Guard and made his infamous statement "when the looting starts, the shooting starts," showing no regard for the reason that some people were rioting. To exacerbate further an already tumultuous time,

---

[52] William Cummings, "Trump Tells Congresswomen to 'Go Back' to the 'Crime Infested Places from Which They Came'," USA Today (Gannett Satellite Information Network, July 15, 2019), https://www.usatoday.com/story/news/politics/2019/07/14/trump-tells-congresswomen-go-back-counties-they-came/1728253001/

when protestors were peacefully marching along Black Lives Matter Blvd. in Lafayette Park near the White House on June 1, 2020, they were met with police in riot gear and the National Guard shooting rubber bullets and tear gas for force them to disperse.

Once the area was cleared, the president walked across Lafayette Park to St. John's Episcopal Church where he stood and held a Bible in the air.

The presiding bishop of the Episcopal Church, Michael Curry, issued a stern statement of rebuke after one of their churches was illicitly used as the backdrop for partisan division:

> This evening, the president of the United States stood in front of St. John's Episcopal Church, lifted up a Bible, and had pictures of himself taken. In so doing, he used a church building and the Holy Bible for partisan political purposes. This was done in a time of deep hurt and pain in our country, and his action did nothing to help us or to heal us.[53]

The Episcopal bishop of Washington, The Right Rev. Mariann Budde, responded in an interview by saying:

> I am outraged. I am the bishop of the Episcopal Diocese of Washington and was not given even a courtesy call [that] they would be clearing the area with tear gas so they could use one of our churches as a prop… Everything he has said and done is to inflame violence. We need moral leadership, and he's done everything to divide us.[54]

The president of the United States used the National Guard to spray teargas and shoot rubber bullets at US citizens protesting the killing of another unarmed Black person by a police officer so that he could stage

---

[53] "Presiding Bishop Michael Curry's Statement on President Donald Trump's Use of St. John's, Holy Bible," Episcopal News Service, June 8, 2020, https://www.episcopalnewsservice.org/pressreleases/presiding-bishop-michael-currys-statement-on-president-donald-trumps-use-of-st-johns-holy-bible/

[54] Sarah Pulliam Bailey Michelle Boorstein, "Episcopal Bishop on President Trump: 'Everything He Has Said and Done Is to Inflame Violence'," The Washington Post (WP Company, June 2, 2020), https://www.washingtonpost.com/religion/bishop-budde-trump-church/2020/06/01/20ca70f8-a466-11ea-b619-3f9133bbb482_story.html

a photo op holding a Bible in front of a church.[55] He, along with an all-white cast of accomplices, posed in front of the church for pictures while the peaceful protestors were tending to their wounds from the rubber bullets, tear gas, and other traumatic effects of the attack.

SENSORY WORK

Tasting the bitter dregs of discomfort when talking about race, racism, and white supremacy is an integral part of the work of doing racial justice. It's hard to get around it. For many white people, it can be uncomfortable and requires a level of vulnerability and honesty that is undesirable. However, we cannot address the truths of racial injustice without having these type of hard conversations.

I invite you to think about a time when you had to broach a subject matter that made you feel uncomfortable, yet you remained in the conversation.

- What strategies did you employ to enable you to stay present and press through the discomfort?
- Could you employ the same strategies when talking with others about race, or do you need to develop new ones?

Think of three people you know with whom you would like to talk about racism.

- Why did you choose these particular people?
- What would you hope to gain from this conversation?
- How might this conversation be a starting point to taking action for racial equality?

* * *

But let justice roll down like waters, and righteousness like an ever-flowing stream. —Amos 5:24

---

[55] "President Trump Orders up Photo Op at Church near White House - CNN Video," CNN (Cable News Network, June 2, 2020), https://www.cnn.com/videos/us/2020/06/02/donald-trump-church-photo-op-george-floyd-protest-bash-pkg-vpx-es.cnn

CHAPTER 5

Holy Boldness

One of the claims that has been made about the impact of the Ferguson uprising on policing is that police became fearful to engage in proactive measures, such as stopping suspicious people, and that as a result, crime rates have increased. This theory has been dubbed the "Ferguson Effect." However, there are other ways to consider the effect of the Ferguson uprising on policing in particular and our society in general.

It is unlikely that the calls for police reform would have garnered the kind of attention from the federal and local governments without the sustained protests in Ferguson. Unfortunately, this was not the first killing of an unarmed Black person by a police officer in the United States. In 1999, New York police officers shot Amadou Diallo nineteen times as he held up his wallet. In 2009, an Oakland, CA, police officer shot Oscar Grant in the back. In 2010, Danroy "DJ" Henry, a college student from Massachusetts, was shot to death through his car window after a Pace University football game. All of these victims were unarmed and their deaths garnered media attention and protests; however, it was the dramatic footage from the streets of Ferguson and the sustained protests following Ferguson that made it difficult to carry on with business as usual. Media outlets were present in Ferguson from around the world, and the story of an unarmed Black teen being killed by police shone a spotlight on the long-standing issue of racial injustice in policing. It is unlikely that the US Attorney General would have traveled to Ferguson or Missouri's governor establishing a commission would have occurred without the sustained protests.

Uncovering and addressing systemic racial inequities in policing should be considered a positive step forward. We should not be content with Black people's names becoming hashtags as a result of police violence. Growing up in New Jersey, I remember the public outcry about racial profiling along the New Jersey Turnpike.[56] Police, sometimes with weapons drawn, were stopping Black motorists, stripping them, and searching their cars, leaving them traumatized and humiliated. This practice was not only happening in New Jersey; Black people from around the country have reported the same issue. And it has not been limited to motorists.

In 2010, Jordan Miles was a senior and a gifted viola player at the Creative and Performing Arts High School in Pittsburgh. On January 12, as he walked a short distance to his grandmother's house, plainclothes police officers who deemed him "suspicious" stopped him. That encounter ended in a brutal beating that left Jordan hospitalized.[57] The officers were not charged with excessive force, and Jordan, once an honor roll and musically gifted student, has understandably struggled to regain his footing after that tragic event.

Enough!

One of the recurring themes from my interviews was that the Ferguson uprising ultimately gave voice to people who were saying "Enough!" Enough of the racial profiling! Enough of the police violence! Enough of the systemic racism that has enshrined racial inequity into the foundation of our society! A "holy boldness" of sorts has emerged on a larger scale that is not easily quieted or drowned out. The Ferguson activists were by no means the first people to exert this type of "holy boldness" in this generation, but it was the first time that such action garnered this type of sustained media attention—and every uprising afterward. Cell phone cameras and social media platforms have been a game changer for the work of racial justice. False narratives can no longer dominate the public consciousness when more truthful ones are being replayed from cell phone-recorded videos. Social media platforms make it possible, for better and for worse, to get "on-the-ground" accounts that largely would have remained obscured. The Ferguson uprising represented a kind of awakening that made visible the relentless determination of a people who were, as Fannie Lou Hamer said, "Sick and tired of being sick and tired."

[56] "N.J. Knew of Racial Profiling for Years," ABC News (ABC News Network, January 7, 2006), https://abcnews.go.com/US/story?id=95406&page=1.

[57] Amber Nicotra, "Mom Says She Didn't Recognize Jordan Miles after Violent Arrest," WTAE (WTAE, March 9, 2014), https://www.wtae.com/article/mom-says-she-didn-t-recognize-jordan-miles-after-violent-arrest/7465423#

Rev. Michelle Higgins, co-chair of Action St. Louis, shares some of her thoughts about the kind of relentlessness and determination that emerged in the tenacious pursuit of justice:

> It's obvious that Black people are more bold about self-determination, and I take seriously that value. But I believe that the Ferguson uprising was itself a manifestation of self-determination, that we would not believe police that demonized Mike Brown. We would not wait and go home when our elders came out and told us "Let's just pray." And, in fact, we have the testimony of some of the clergy who first came out in Ferguson. They changed their whole message after they saw the true truth, and that itself was what people of faith would say the Holy Spirit [was] showing them.
>
> The righteous thing that came from the Ferguson uprising is that Black people and people of color around the world realized that, if we want liberation, we are in charge of it. We have to get it. We have to do it our damn selves. And there's actually no way around that. Stacey Abrams's campaign is a clear picture of it. Andrew Gillum's decision to unconcede. And if anything that Ferguson and St. Louis has shown people, whether it was on behalf of Alton Sterling, Philando Castile, shootings in Chicago, BYP 100 (Black Youth Project), and the work that's happening there. They're saying "You know, I might never be safe, but I'm done being afraid." And I think that's what the Ferguson uprising did for us. And that's the Bible.
>
> That's why I stay in it because, when people decide to be fearless, even though they're clearly not safe, they're literally walking in the valley of the shadow of death. That's like the first thing you learn when you're a baby in the church. You say you fear no evil no matter where you are. So that's what helps us to counter and to challenge and to tell it: "No. You go to hell. You go. I live here."

Rev. Julie Taylor, a Unitarian Universalist (UU) chaplain and activist, shares her perspective of the Ferguson uprising on the denomination:

I do not believe we would be where we are right now as
[the] Unitarian Universalist Association if it was not for
Ferguson and the Ferguson uprising. This would not have
happened if those young people had gone home. If those
young people had not stayed on the streets in mourning and
demanded the ability and freedom to mourn. If that had not
happened, our denomination would not be looking at our
own structural racism the way it is. I one hundred percent
believe this because Mike Brown's death brought into such
clear focus the racism, the systemic pieces of racism in this
country as it connects to power in ways that shook enough
of us that it then sparked Baltimore. It sparked Standing
Rock. It sparked a larger piece of consciousness that I think
broke open. For a lot of us that are white, it broke open
the ability to recognize what's been in front of us the whole
time. Fortunately, enough of us in our denomination that
are white broke wide enough open to be willing to bear our
own comfortability that it's going to require us to actually
make the change we keep claiming we want to make in the
world.

Ferguson ignited a new way

Rev. Traci Blackmon, associate general minister of Justice &
Local Church Ministries for The United Church of Christ, shares her
observations of how the Ferguson uprising inspired people to claim
their voice of being "enough" and not diminishing themselves for the
sake of others:

When the Ferguson uprising began, I was pastoring a church
in Florissant, which is about three miles from where Michael
Brown was killed, and I was also working at a local hospital
doing healthcare in the community and was pretty happy
doing those things—thinking I was making a difference in
the places I was in service, and I still believe I was. Because
of the work at the church, [by invitation] I ended up in
Ferguson when Michael Brown died..., and things changed
pretty rapidly from there. I now serve in leadership for my
denomination.

It really—it has changed me spiritually, and it has changed me emotionally. It has changed me mentally. It has reoriented what I believe church to be and how I believe church is to be executed. And I think those things are all necessary in this time. It's expanded my understanding of God and who God is, and it's strengthened my faith and resolve, and my commitment to work out my faith in ways that make a difference in society for those who are inside the church and outside of the church. I think Ferguson has done that.

I was looking at the swearing-in ceremonies for the 2016 elections in the House, and thought not many people, if any, would make this connection, I made a connection to Ferguson for that because I believe that Ferguson is the place where people finally internalized that your economic condition, your racial category, your ethnicity—none of that can take your voice, and your voice is still powerful.

I believe that Ferguson ignited a new way. Not that it had never happened before, but it ignited a new way of people standing up and saying "No! I won't take this. I don't have to take this anymore." And I make a connection to so many women of various faiths and lived experiences being sworn into the House. And not just women but also men. Muslim women were sworn in. Native American women were sworn in. Openly binary-challenging women were sworn in. On multiple books of faith. I think that all of that has to do with the rise of resistance that really took hold in Ferguson. It has morphed into other things and shown up in other places, but this persistent rise of the people's voice that happened in Ferguson, I think, resonates all over this country.

And it's not just that there were women and men of diverse backgrounds but [that] the women really have the spotlight now, and they were there as themselves, and that was enough. The Ferguson effect is being enough. It's not this need to show up in a conforming way. So I was celebrating the fact that a Muslim woman shows up in her hijab. A Palestinian congresswoman shows up in a Palestinian dress. Women showed up with their children. They did this [as if they] were saying, "This is who I am. This is all of who I am. I'm going to be sworn in on a Koran even if that makes you uncomfortable, because this is who I am." What happened in Ferguson is [that] respectability politics did not govern, and that's the thing I see continuing. There was a time when women would have perhaps been able to be sworn into these positions, but we would have shown up in a Brooks Brothers suit. So what I'm particularly attributing to Ferguson is that Ferguson said who I am is enough. And you don't get to diminish me just because of who I am. No matter what narratives you write, no matter what you say, we're here, and we're not going anywhere. That's the Ferguson effect, and it has created a different narrative in this country.

Ferguson will not get ultimate credit for this though because this country rewrites its narratives, but that is the truth of what has happened.

It's so important to be who you are, which is something from Ferguson that has had an impact on me because there was a time when I would play those games of trying to conform my being to fit into spaces so I could be a part of things. I don't play those games anymore, and I don't do that anymore. Even though it's at a great cost, I'm going to be who I am. And I'm going to make space for other people, but I'm not going to shrink. I just won't do that anymore. That's something else I learned from Ferguson.

No Activist Tourism

The General Assembly of the Presbyterian Church (USA) displayed a kind of "Holy boldness" action that was unprecedented in their history when they met in St. Louis in 2018. Their prophetic actions evolved out of their willingness to adapt responsively and follow the nudging of the local faith leaders and join the ongoing efforts for racial justice.

Rev. Dr. Deborah Krause is the president of Eden Seminary in St. Louis and an ordained Presbyterian (PCUSA) clergyperson. During the Ferguson uprising, she was the academic dean at Eden and actively engaged in the movement for racial justice. She recalls the historic General Assembly that met in St. Louis in 2018 and the groundwork that was laid for attendees to learn about and participate in a justice initiative in St. Louis and return home with the capacity to join into the struggle for racial justice in their own communities:

The General Assembly of the Presbyterian Church (USA) gathered in St. Louis for our biennial meeting in June of 2018. The leadership of the Presbyterian Church came to town two years ahead of time and wanted to kind of get a taste of Ferguson. There is a leader here in St. Louis who was the moderator of our Presbytery, Erin Counihan. And Erin came to St. Louis in August of 2014, just as the Ferguson uprising was starting to happen. And she's the pastor at Oak Hill Presbyterian Church, and she was the only one of other Presbyterians who was actively engaged on the street. And here she was, brand new, in her thirties, didn't know a soul, and I was really impressed by her. She's a phenomenal leader and ended up getting nominated to be the moderator of our Presbytery. That's unheard of for somebody to be that new and move into leadership like that. But it was the appropriate call, and the Spirit really was moving when she was elected.

As the moderator of the Presbytery, she had particular power and authority to help shape how the GA would be embodied here. I came to know Erin through some Presbyterian interaction but mostly through protests. She was very active in the Stockley protests and very much a part of the kind of #expectus religious leadership group that was engaged with Stockley. She has a lot of credibility across the religious leader and activist spectrum in St. Louis, and she was just brilliant. It was great to watch her and to collaborate with her in directing the folks from Louisville, which is our national office, to move from "We're going to come to St. Louis and build a Habitat house, and that's how we'll get the GA participants involved in St. Louis."

We said, "You know, housing is a huge issue in St. Louis, but we want you to pay attention to how structural injustice is embodied here." And they'd had a little bit of that when they were at the Detroit General Assembly two years prior, so they were kind of ready to engage. We said, "You're not going to do activist tourism here. We're going to work with you to identify an issue that the social justice community after Ferguson, after Stockley, is working on here to really impact criminal justice reform. And we're going to bring the GA into solidarity with that."

We talked to several local activists and identified the Close the Workhouse initiative, which is trying to close the medium-security city jail. It is essentially a debtors' prison. It is a medium-security jail where people who can't afford to pay the bail on their warrants can end up ...[for] a week to a month or longer. And it's dreadful. It doesn't have adequate heating and cooling. It's full of rats, cockroaches, and black mold. It's a dungeon, and the security in it is very poor. People are physically assaulted all the time. It is an infamous hellhole and has been for decades. But the criminal justice reform activists, who've been particularly strengthened through the Ferguson movement and through Stockley, had been organizing to close it and, with that, to end cash bail in St. Louis City and St. Louis County. We worked with those local activists who are in those campaigns to educate the General Assembly about that, because cash bail is a system that is integrated into racial inequity and criminal justice inequality across our country.

Close the Workhouse protest at the Federal Building in Downtown St. Louis *(Photo by Erin Counihan)*

We saw this as something they can learn about here in St. Louis, but then you can take this home and you can work on it in your town. You can take it to your church and begin to do power mapping in your local community, attend [to] how these practices are present in your community, and decide particular ways you can move as a church to witness against them and to get them changed. We ended up getting almost the entire General Assembly population, thousands and thousands of people, marching in the city of St. Louis to end cash bail, and by the end of it, more than $50,000 that had been raised to bail people out of jail.

I do not think that a mainline denomination has done anything like that as a public witness. J. Herbert Nelson, the moderator of the Church, was very brave. He put his national leadership on the line to do that. And he had been the biggest advocate of doing a Habitat for Humanity house, but he pivoted and adjusted. He listened. He learned. He moved, and he spoke with such passion and eloquence on the steps of the city jail. He was great. I think it's the only time that there has been an action like that associated with a General Assembly, and I don't think there'll be another in which they don't do some sort of public action to move the people there and get them involved in the issues to make an impact in that city.

Watching this young Presbyterian minister who knew how to work her relationships and authority in the local Presbytery was amazing. She took herself seriously enough to be the moderator of the church, and that positioned her then to leverage her relationships nationally, and to get to collaborate with her in that is an example of what religious leadership can be in relationship to social justice work. There was a protest involved in this, but it was organizing. It wasn't just going out in the street and making a big noise. It was all done with the intention of getting Presbyterian people into a space to put their bodies out there in a way that was tied to an actual issue that we were all working on, that we had studied and prepared for, and that we had raised money for. Our leaders spoke against this system, and we all committed to fighting the system in our local churches and spaces and Presbytery. They created a massive demonstration that brought a lot of public attention to this. They certainly got the City of St. Louis to think differently about its tourism convention relationships. This big convention was activated to go into the street and protest the city. I mean it was just amazing, and this the kind of thing that the church can begin to see itself in that more sort of trickster space. There is vitality in that. We don't have to be conformed to this world. We have a calling and an opportunity to live into the Kingdom of God.

General Assembly of the PCUSA protest in St. Louis
in June, 2018. *(Photo by Danny Bolin)*

The protest didn't end with the closing prayer of the General Assembly. The hope was for the participants to take what they had learned and apply it to an issue in their local contexts. One of the ways that happened was the extension of the end cash bail effort into Louisville, Kentucky, the headquarters for the PCUSA. Dr. Nelson led another march the following year in Louisville to continue to draw attention to the injustice of cash bail. They formally partnered with The Bail Project whose mission is to end cash bail and create a more just pretrial system.[58] On August 24–30, 2020, the PCUSA hosted a

---

[58] "The Bail Project." The Bail Project, April 14, 2020, https://bailproject. org/

Week of Action to End Systemic Racism in Louisville. The vision and purpose of the activities were outlined on their website:

> It is abundantly clear through the gospel narrative and the greater witness of the Bible, that God has called us, as people of faith, to seek justice for those most marginalized in our world. As a Matthew 25 denomination, it is the vision of our church to eradicate white supremacy and dismantle institutionalized racism. Furthermore, in an effort to do the "hands & feet" work the Lord ordains, we must act and bear witness to the gospel in these crucial times.

Rev. Dr. J. Herbert Nelson, II, stated clerk of the General Assembly of the Presbyterian Church (USA), speaking at the rally in St. Louis to end cash bail. *(Photo by Jennifer Jones)*

The PCUSA staff expressed a deep yearning to be more engaged in responding to the murders of Breonna Taylor, Tony McDade, George Floyd, Ahmaud Arbery, and countless others who died at the hands of the police and racism. From this need has come the "Bearing Witness" working group, which has participation from the Presbyterian Mission Agency, Office of the General Assembly, Administrative Services Group, and Presbyterian Publishing Corporation. From this group a number of strategies are being formulated to provide advocacy campaigns, education initiatives, and opportunities to join with community efforts organized by the Movement for Black Lives, Louisville Showing Up for Racial Justice, The Bail Project, and other grassroots groups.

As a centerpiece of this movement, we will host a *Presbyterian Week of Action*. This endeavor is structured to provide a public witness that facilitates education, visibility, and action that reinforces our PCUSA statements and policy around the support of eradicating racism and acknowledging that God loves all Black lives. By joining together as national staff and the greater church, we hope to provide faithful leadership in the area of justice, love, and equality within our denomination and communities.[59]

From webinars and Bible studies to a COVID-19 memorial service and day of service, the church called the community to join their efforts of drawing attention to racial injustice and working to eradicate it. During the justice rally on August 29, one of the speakers was the president of Louisville Presbyterian Seminary, Rev. Dr. Alton Pollard. Rev. Dr. Pollard pointed out that six months after Breonna Taylor's murder, there still was no justice and that therefore the struggle for justice continued. He connected this struggle to the historic struggle for racial justice in America and offered a poignant list of demands:

- We demand justice for Breonna Taylor, her family, and all who love her.
- We reject non-solutions, hollow answers, outright deceptions, and formulaic responses.
- We demand an end to the carceral state in Black and brown communities.
- We demand an end to economic apartheid in our cities.
- We demand an end to inequitable healthcare everywhere.
- We demand an end to the devaluing and dehumanization of entire peoples.
- We demand an end to the devastation of our planet.
- Until the winds of justice blow everywhere, we will not be satisfied.[60]

[59] "Presbyterian Week of Action." Presbyterian Church (U.S.A.) (Presbyterian Church (U.S.A.), July 31, 2020), https://www.pcusa.org/weekofaction/

[60] "Dr. Alton Pollard's speech at the Presbyterian Rally for Justice." YouTube Video, August 29, 2020, https://www.youtube.com/watch?v=q4ADrzCih-8

Rev. Dr. Alton Pollard, president of Louisville Presbyterian Seminary,
giving a speech at the justice rally on August 29, 2020. *(Photo by Chris Wooten)*

Protests calling for justice for Breonna Taylor continued for months in Louisville in
2020. Left to right: Keturah Herron, Travis Nagdy, Pastor F. Bruce Williams, Pastor
Timothy Finley, and Rev. Stachelle Bussey

Travis Nagdy, a leader in the movement for Justice for Breonna,
was tragically killed on November 23, 2020. *(Photo by Ty TakingPhotos)*

Rev. Krista Taves was the pastor of Emerson Unitarian Universalist Chapel during the Ferguson uprising and is now serving two UU congregations in other states. This is her story of continuing the work of racial justice in her new congregations:

> A few months after our interview, I actually announced to the congregation that I was resigning. Within less than a year after Michael Brown's shooting, I was no longer in service at the Emerson Unitarian Universalist Chapel. I still live in the St. Louis area, and I serve two congregations. I serve a congregation in Quincy, Illinois and in LaCrosse, Wisconsin.
>
> There was a great deal of conflict happening in the congregation even before the shooting. I think the Ferguson uprising added another level of anxiety to congregational life. And my very strong involvement in the protest movement at that time received mixed feedback from the congregation. It wasn't the only thing going on, but it added to the anxiety, and it became impossible for me to be effective as their minister. So I resigned.
>
> One of the things that did happen that I'm very pleased about was the vigil we started in Chesterfield. The vigil continued on, and it's still going every Saturday. In fact, the leaders of the vigil at Emerson decided to take it and turn it into its own organization outside of the congregation and invite non-Unitarians and local people from West County.
>
> So there's now an organization called WE CAN (West Country Community Action Network). It is now its own organization with its own board of directors, and this organization has multiple facets. They've worked specifically with the Kirkwood Public School system to change the disciplinary practices and bring ... a racial equity lens, especially around out-of-school suspensions, and they've made some significant inroads there. They also work with the Chesterfield Police Department bringing anti-racism and equity training to the police department as well as addressing their use of force policies and really encouraging local police departments to bring in de-escalation training. They decided that they needed to go and be active in West County. West County being [the]

predominately white center of economic power in the St. Louis area. This is where they needed to focus their energy, so that's what they've done.

Mostly what I have done is taken my experience and my passion to my two other congregations. The Quincy, Illinois, congregation is a small congregation with about sixty members. We recently did a program through Meadville Lombard [Seminary] called "Beloved Conversations." We did an eight-week intensive program, so we have a core of leaders in the congregation who are very committed to being ready, when needed in Quincy, to be a voice for racial equity. Quincy is about 96 percent white; however, there is an African American community that's been there since Quincy started, and it's actually quite cohesive. I've been able to build relationships in Quincy that, in St. Louis, seemed elusive, because it's such a small community of only 40,000 people. In St. Louis, it is also much more racially segregated, and I feel like the divide in St. Louis is actually wider to cross that line [than] it is in Quincy. I find that I've been able to cross that line much more easily, and the members of the congregation help me to do that. How you go about building trust is everything. I had people from the congregation who invited me into relationships with leaders in the African American community who have now become friends.

There was a core of social justice-minded folks in the congregation who had been watching what was going on in St. Louis. They were listening and getting a lot of information about what was going on and wondering what their part in it was. When I first got the job during the one-year anniversary of Michael Brown's death, I hadn't

even met any of them yet, and I just said, "Look, I'm going to be taking part in the year anniversary marches and actions, and anybody who wants to join me from Quincy, I'd love to meet you." And five people came. I hadn't even met them yet, and those people became the central leaders in doing the anti-racism training that we did in my second year with them.

In La Crosse, it's also a predominately white congregation of about ninety people. However, there was a core group who did a book study, *Waking up White* by Debby Irving. This is a covenant group that dedicated an entire year to this book. And they decided that their mission was to continue this work in the congregation at large. Now, they're in their third year, and it's called BCOR, Beloved Conversations Opposing Racism, and they are actively building relationships with each other and leaders of color in La Crosse.

There is also a significant Native American population around La Crosse—the Ho-Chunk nation and other people that have affiliated with that nation. Our congregation has worked to become a reliable ally or organization in solidarity with the Ho-Chunk people for the purposes of elevating and augmenting their voice and influence in the community and responding to their issues. So those are the two areas of focused racial equity in La Crosse that the congregation has been working on.

Jake Lyonfields is co-leader of WE CAN and a member at Emerson Unitarian Universalist Chapel. He describes how he entered this work and the ways in which the group continues its public witness throughout the St. Louis region:

I grew up in West County St. Louis and went to college at Washington University. During college and afterwards, I was active in my congregation, Emerson Unitarian Universalist Chapel, which is located out in West County, a more affluent, whiter suburb. I was becoming a leader in my congregation, serving on the board and in different capacities. Krista, I found, was a very empowering figure in all that. I graduated in May of 2014 from my undergraduate program and continued to be part of my congregation. Then I began to be involved in work related to municipal court reform, which, of course, once the uprising happened, became an issue that garnered national attention.

When I was searching for my people after college, I knew I wanted to do justice work. I had deep roots in issues related to environmental sustainability and environmental justice. But I hadn't worked more directly on the local or regional level around transforming systems and addressing their systemic racism. Two or three months after the Ferguson uprising had begun, we still didn't know what to do. Our social justice team within our church seemed to be going around in circles, and eventually there was a call to action by Rev. Taves to stand on a street corner with signs that said "Black Lives Matter" in the city in which we worshiped. Everyone was quite nervous about it, but we showed up on the corner of one of the largest contiguous malls in America in Chesterfield, Missouri, with signs that said "Black Lives Matter." We showed up the next week and the week after that.

We found that this was an extremely disruptive thing to do in a city that is ninety percent white and incredibly affluent. It was disruptive for folks who would pass by our vigils. We called them vigils because we were witnessing for racial justice. Not only was it disruptive for folks who passed by, we also found it to be disruptive for ourselves. This was an opportunity for folks to stand on a street corner at a major intersection holding up signs, engaging with one another about work, education, and being in community with ourselves, which helped us bolster our identity as community organizers. It empowered participants in those vigils to understand themselves within the context of what was going on and understand their role. We thought this was something that we could do for a couple of months then stop. We set a deadline for doing these vigils, but that deadline came and went. We set another deadline for doing these vigils, and that deadline came and went. We realized that we didn't want to stop, and here we are, four-and-a-half years later, and we've missed maybe three or four Saturdays in all those years. We've since expanded our vigils so that we're not just in Chesterfield every Saturday but we rotate and have these vigils in other white, affluent areas of West County.

The vigils have become something that is integral to our work for witnessing for racial justice, but it is also as much about maintaining the sense of community that sustains our work because we've expanded to include police reform, school discipline reform, and voting rights reform. We've expanded our work to pursue systems-level change, but we also understand ourselves to be sort of deferent to some of the same leaders and some of the organizations that have emerged from the Ferguson uprising.

WE CAN volunteers before for a
Saturday vigil. *(Photo by Jake Lyonfields)*

WE CAN Volunteers continued protesting
through the pandemic. *(Photo by Ashley Kuykendall)*

One of our guiding principles is that we are going to follow the lead of Black leaders and the Ferguson Commission report. We planned to use that report and those individuals as our guiding stars in our work because we knew it was our responsibility, as a majority white organization, to continue witnessing for racial justice and engaging other white folks.

However, we also needed to make sure that we were held accountable to these organizations that were at the helm of this local movement and what has become a national movement.

For our organization, WE CAN (West County Community Action Network), accountability looks like a couple of different things. The most prominent example is that in everything we do—our goals for our organizing teams, for example—are informed by the call to action in the Ferguson Commission report. We've been pursuing police reform within municipal police departments and are seeking changes outlined as calls to action in the report. Eliminating pre-K through third grade out-of-school suspensions is a major call to action in the report. So that's largely how it informs our work.

We are really proud of the intergenerational aspect of our organization. One of the ways we have grown is that we've established a formal leadership team. I was one of the de facto leaders along with other folks, but it became apparent that as our membership grew and our work expanded, we needed to create a more formal governing structure. We are majority white, and that's a function, in part, of where we do our work in West County, which is an overwhelmingly white area. I also think it's a function of the fact that this work is stressful and people of color are dealing with it every single day. It's incumbent upon us as white folks to do the work and engage our white counterparts in our community. I am also quite certain that, when people of color engage in multiracial racial justice work, working in partnership with white folks certainly can be exhausting. We've had incidents of racism manifesting in our organization, and I don't want erase that. But we are a group of happy, excited folks who are doing this work, and I just love our community so dearly. It's become a really significant part of my life.

Racial justice resistance during Covid-19

"This is the day the Lord has made and we will rejoice and be glad in it!" I cheerily recited this familiar Call to Worship during the Christian Theological Seminary chapel service on March 4, 2020. After a few more pleasantries, the instructions that followed were something I had never given before. "Today, we are going to pass the peace and celebrate Communion a little differently. There are growing concerns about the coronavirus that was discovered in China and is making its way to the US. So instead of hugs and handshakes during the passing of the peace, please clasp your hands in a prayer position and nod at the person you are greeting. I think it's best that we don't touch each other. For Communion, the servers will wash their hands and tear off a piece of bread for each person, and you can wave that piece over the Communion cup in lieu of dipping." These instructions were met with a few quizzical looks and a couple of snickers. Some people complied but many just carried on as usual, especially during the passing of the peace. Little did we know how drastically our lives were about to change.

Earlier that week, I had turned the page on my kitchen calendar from February to March. This is a *Simple Inspirations* wall calendar with colorful artwork by Debi Hron and thought-provoking sayings to encourage you along the journey. The artwork above the March calendar was a giant heart, surrounded by colorful flowers on a Black background, which framed the words "Keep some room in your heart for the unimaginable." I gasped when I read these words. "What happened to the joyful, heartwarming messages?" I said to myself. I don't want to have to reserve room for the *unimaginable*, which I also interpreted as the unthinkable, which usually isn't good.

I never imagined that as dean of Christian Theological Seminary I would immediately have to transition our school to online learning. I didn't anticipate that I would get a text from one of our son's school saying they were closing that day, and jump up from a meeting and say, "I have to go now!" It never occurred to me that the March 23 to April 4 trip to China with our oldest son's Mandarin class, which we had been planning for the past two years, would never come to pass. The list of challenges and disappointments goes on and on, but most importantly, COVID-19 created an *unimaginable* amount of sickness and death and, unfortunately, it still is. The global pandemic that created the largest health, economic, and educational crisis in this era was nothing that I ever imagined, and the horrific response by the president of the United States exacerbated the spread of the virus. We soon earned our title as the world leader in COVID-19 infections and deaths. I never would have imagined that a president would politicize a health crisis, since a virus will aggressively infect any available human. The president downplayed the virus by first claiming it to be a hoax, then said that it would go away soon, then refusing to wear a mask, then insisting that businesses, schools, and houses of worship open up much sooner than advisable, then mocked the scientists and tampered with the CDC reporting. All of this led to a stark political divide between who was wearing a mask and social distancing and who wasn't. As a result, the US retained its top-tier place of worldwide COVID-19 infections and deaths as health systems became overwhelmed and patients lay sick and dying alone in hospitals as their loved ones' grief was compounded by the distance.

The COVID-19 pandemic and its ensuing economic and educational devastation, coupled with the tragic death of Kobe Bryant, his daughter Gianna, and nine others in a helicopter crash, was enough to make 2020 an *unimaginable* year of pain and suffering. However, there was more to come. Breonna Taylor, an EMT technician, was killed by police who burst unannounced into her home in the middle of the night. Breonna's boyfriend, who had a licensed gun, jumped out of bed to try and protect them, but could not from the more than thirty bullets that entered their apartment.

There were no illegal items found in Breonna's home. The intel that the officers used was obviously flawed, and nobody has been prosecuted for killing Breonna. The Louisville community rose up in righteous anger. Activists, clergy, and everyday people maintained justice actions for months in an attempt to secure justice for Breonna, although there has been none to be found. A picture of her in her work uniform while smiling sweetly is etched in my mind.

It was also around this time that we learned about Ahmaud Arbery, a young Black man jogging in Brunswick, Georgia, whom neighborhood racists killed in February for looking suspicious. This tragedy was similar to what happened to Trayvon Martin, the seventeen-year-old in Sanford, Florida, who was walking home from the store when a neighborhood racist who thought he was "up to no good" stalked and killed him. Similar to Trayvon, weeks passed before Ahmaud's killing gained national attention, and the perpetrators were not arrested until a national spotlight of shame was shone on these situations.

In May 2020, we witnessed the video of George Floyd being arrested in Minneapolis for *allegedly* passing a counterfeit $20 bill in a local store. A store employee called the police and George was handcuffed and detained on the ground beside a police car. As he lay handcuffed on the city street, an officer pressed his knee on George's neck for 8 minutes and 46 seconds. George's pleas for help and relief went unanswered, and we watched him lie there and die. It was too much for us to bear. Remember, it was in the Minneapolis area in 2016 that police pulled over Philando Castile, the Montessori school cafeteria supervisor who knew every child by name. Though he notified the police officer that he had a licensed gun in the car as he kept his hands on the steering wheel, the officer shot him to death while his girlfriend filmed the entire incident and her young daughter watched from the back seat. Protests occurred all over the city and gained nationwide attention. The Montessori schoolchildren even held their own protest march to seek justice for their beloved Mr. Phil.

Now just a few years later, the public execution of George Floyd confronted the city. Floyd's killing sparked major protests that resulted in the burning of a Minneapolis police station. The video made clear that there had been no reason for the police officer to restrain him that way, and that his resulting death was too much to bear. The rage and outrage was seen and heard around the world. Almost every major city held a large protest to call for justice for George Floyd and express outrage at the ongoing killing of unarmed Black people by police officers in the so-called civilized and enlightened USA.

Not only were we confronted with the raging COVID-19 pandemic, we now were reeling with the effects of the recent killing of George Floyd, Breonna Taylor, and Ahmaud Arbery. It was *unimaginable*. However, I could imagine Indianapolis joining the nationwide efforts to protest these killings and call for justice. Pentecost Sunday was a few days away, and it seemed apropos for a faith-led march for racial justice on that sacred day. I reached out to Shoshanna Spector at Faith in Indiana to see if they would be interested organizing a protest march, and she enthusiastically said yes. The next thing I knew, Faith in Indiana organizers and I were moving full steam ahead to organize a "Processions for Racial Justice" in just a few days. Shoshanna, Rosie Bryant, and Nicole Barnes were helping make logistical and tactical plans and we texted and talked more times than I can count over those few days. Rev. Ivan Hicks, pastor of First Baptist Church in Indianapolis, and other faith leaders brought in others to join the effort and help out wherever needed.

Philando Castile burial site, Calvary Cemetery,
St. Louis *(Photo by Leah Gunning Francis)*

A short program was organized to kick off the march. Local faith leaders spoke briefly and passionately about the need for racial justice and police reform. With an estimated one thousand people in tow, we donned our face masks and marched from the Indiana State Capitol to the City-County building and held a die-in. Participants lay down on the ground or wherever they could find a spot, while Faith in Indiana organizer Nicole Barnes and I read the names of one hundred unarmed Black people that had been killed by police nationwide over the past several years.

Images from the George Floyd March in Indianapolis
on Pentecost Sunday, May 31, 2020.

Faith leaders gathered on the steps of the
Indiana State Capitol. *(Photos by Carrie Hettle)*

Protestors gather at the Indiana State Capitol. *(Photos by Jerrel Farries)*

Protestors march from the Indiana State Capital to the
City-County building. *(Photos by Carrie Hettle)*

Protestors march from the Indiana State Capital to the
City-County building. *(Photos by Carrie Hettle)*

Protestors march from the Indiana State Capital to the City-County building. *(Photos by Carrie Hettle)*

Rabbi Brett Krichiver, senior rabbi at Indianapolis Hebrew Congregation, speaks before the die-in. *(Photo by Carrie Hettle)*

Protestors point toward the mayor's office as the list of police reform demands are read. *(Photo by Jerrel Farries)*

Protestors participate in the die-in. *(Photo by Jerrel Farries)*

Nicole Barnes reads 100 names of Black people killed by police as protestors lie on the ground for 8 minutes and 46 seconds. *(Photo by Jerrel Farries)*

Eric Garner...

Atatiana Jefferson...

Emantic "EJ" Bradford, Jr. ...

Gregory Edwards...

Antwon Rose...

Stephon Clark...

Bettie Jones...

Aaron Bailey...

Dreasjon Reed...

Charleena Lyles...

Jordan Edwards...

Indianapolis musician Tony Artis struck his large jembe drum after each name was read. One hundred names. One hundred drum beats that honored each life.

Tony Artis struck his drum after each name was read
during the die-in. *(Photo by Jerrel Farries)*

The die-in lasted 8 minutes and 46 seconds, in memory of the time that George Floyd lay dying on the Minneapolis street, without any help being tendered him. One of the distinctions about this particular die-in is that many, if not all, of the people who participate actually saw the image or watched the video of George Floyd laying constrained on a city street and pleading for relief until his breathing stopped. We watched a man die, and it was too much to bear.

SENSORY WORK

Holy boldness shows up in courageous actions that emerge from a place of profound conviction and sheer will. The kind of fearlessness that Michelle Higgins and Traci Blackmon describe, and the persistence that Deb Krause describes reflect this kind of energy.

I invite you to consider your own "final straw" that may lead you to acts of holy boldness:

- What is the demarcation line related to racial justice that, if crossed, would inspire you to say "Enough!"?
- Has it already been reached and if so, what has it prompted you to do?
- If not, how might you respond?
- What kind of support do you think you would need to act on your feelings?
- How does this particular issue relate to other areas of your life?
- Can you identify others that are doing work in response to your "final straw" that you would like to do? How might you join them?

* * *

When justice is done, it brings joy to the righteous but terror to evildoers. – Proverbs 21:15 (NIV)

Aerial view of die-in on May 31, 2020. *(Photo by Aaron Phillips)*

CHAPTER 6

·························

Finding Joy

There are moments that the words don't reach
There is suffering to terrible to name
You hold your child as tight as you can
And push away the unimaginable
— Lin-Manuel Miranda

"It's Quiet Uptown," *Hamilton*

Rabbi Susan Talve has served as the founding rabbi of Central Reform Congregation for more than thirty years. Throughout her tenure, she has embedded herself in the work of fighting against racism and poverty in St. Louis and advocating for the well-being of children and families. For years, she has shown up at street vigils around St. Louis when someone has been killed by gun violence, serving as a source of comfort and care for the loved ones of the deceased during their time of pain and sorrow. On January 12, 2018, Rabbi Talve and her husband, Rabbi James Stone Goodman, were faced with the unimaginable grief that no parent wants to endure. Their beloved daughter, Adina Talve-Goodman, died at thirty-one years old, and left their family to have to live brokenhearted with the unimaginable.

As described in early chapters, Rabbi Talve was actively involved in the Ferguson uprising and remained engaged in many protests and justice-oriented actions in the years following. She was deeply connected with many people in the protest movements, and she describes her protest family's response on the day of Adina's funeral.

> When it turned out that my daughter's funeral had to be on that Monday of Dr. King's birthday, I knew that it wouldn't

be a good day for my protest family to show up because there are so many other things for them to show up to that day, to honor Dr. King and the legacy of nonviolent resistance to racism. And yet, when I looked out at the thousand people that showed up, that's who I saw. I saw my protest family there.

Traci [Blackmon] sang *Amazing Grace* and *Swing Low, Sweet Chariot* at my daughter's funeral because that's what Adina would have wanted. She knew the history of that song and she cared about that. My daughter's life was about being a body of difference and speaking for bodies of difference. She had just turned thirty-one when she died, and in her thirty years of living, she taught me how to be radically present. She demanded it of me. As a little girl she would take my head in her hands and say, "Mommy, I am talking to you. Pay attention." She taught me to pay attention, to be radically present. And I think we need that today. We can't afford to hide.

When Trump was elected and we were all so devastated, I called Adina. She sent me a video of Maya Angelou reading her poem "And Still I Rise." I've kept that message on my phone, and every once in a while, I've gotta hear Maya reminding us to choose life every day. To choose life and be so radically present that you don't miss anybody and that nobody's invisible and everybody matters. And when we lose a life, we lose a whole world. We are so much less complete, and we have so much more work to do to fill that space. When I think about all the people who have lost children to gun violence and to things that didn't need to happen, it's devastating. And I know how broken I am and how hard it is to breathe life into every day and choose life. Maybe that's why the world is so broken ... because so many of us are so broken.

The radical presence that the protest family demonstrated that somber day grew out of the relationships and care that have been cultivated over their time of shared purpose and commitment. Genuine friendships have developed. Relationships with people with whom they likely would never have connected been forged. New acquaintances have been made. And in times of difficulty like this, the lines of friend and family become blurred to see everyone a family in heart and spirit.

There have been several Ferguson activists as well as those in other cities that have died over the past seven years. Many of them have died under highly suspicious circumstances:

Darren Seals, 29, Ferguson

Deandre Joshua, 20, Ferguson

Edward Crawford, Jr., 27, Ferguson

MarShawn McCarrel, 23, Ferguson

Danye Jones, 24, Ferguson

Bassem Masri, 31, Ferguson

Rev. Carlton Lee, 34, Ferguson

Kris Smith, 42, Louisville

Hamza "Travis" Nagdy, 21, Louisville

Caleb Reed, 17, Chicago

The poem that Rabbi Talve references, "Still I Rise" by Dr. Maya Angelou, has been a source of inspiration and hope for many over the years. Its themes of perseverance and hope have inspired many to face pain-filled days with a belief that they can get through it. You can see a video recording of Dr. Angelou reciting this inspiring poem at the link footnoted below.[61]

What Can I Do? What Can't You Do!

"What can I do?" is a question I hear frequently in lectures and presentations. One day the question came from a woman in an affluent congregation as she wondered aloud about the improbability of any action making a dent in the massive problem of racial injustice.

---

[61] And Still I Rise, YouTube (YouTube, 2007), https://www.youtube.com/watch?v=JqOqo50LSZ0.

It was in that moment that I had a sort of epiphany—not because I had not heard the question before, but because of the space in which the question was posed. As I sat in this well-endowed, well-kept, and well-connected church, I began to wonder aloud about what she *couldn't* do. There was something about sitting in this beautiful and expansive space that invited me to imagine a plethora of possibilities. I wonder if the question "What can *I* do?" is the wrong question to ask. For that question often leads us down a road of examples of failed initiatives and seemingly insignificant actions that cause people to throw their hands up and declare "There's nothing I can do!" I suggest we ask a new question: "What *can't* I do?"

The "What *can't* I do?" question challenges us to take a closer look at the gifts, resources, and opportunities in front of us and *imagine* the countless ways we can put them to use. This question challenges us to start from a place of abundance—to take stock of all of the resources we often take for granted and begin to see our opportunities for making a difference as being as numerous as the stars in the sky. If we survey our personal and communal landscapes from a starting point of abundance, we position ourselves as agents ready to join God's work of repairing and restoring a world fractured by racial injustice.

Shifting from "What can *I* do?" to "What *can't* I do?" not only changes our point of view, it emboldens us to move from helplessness to hope, passivity to possibility, and apathy to action. Perhaps the next time you are tempted to succumb to the "What can *I* do?" posture, take a closer look at what is in front of you, around you, and inside you, and you just might see a whole new world of possibilities before you.

"This doesn't come with a brochure"

Rev. Michael Kinman was the dean at Christ Church Cathedral during the Ferguson uprising, and has since become the rector of All Saints Church in Pasadena, California. He shares his story of moving to a new church and the familiar work that awaited him in California:

> There was a piece of moving out of the context of St. Louis and Ferguson that was especially hard because of what happened and what we shared there. I moved to Pasadena in 2016 to serve as rector of All Saints Church, and about a month before I arrived, an unarmed Black man named

Reginald "JR" Thomas, Jr. had been killed by a Pasadena police officer. The community was in the process of trying to figure out how to respond, and this was on the heels of another killing. In 2012, a young man named Kendrec McDade, an unarmed college student, was shot to death by a Pasadena police officer. In 2017, twenty-one-year-old Christopher Ballew was brutally beaten to the point of breaking his leg after being stopped for allegedly having illegal tinted windows.

Part of what I recognized ..., as I watched this community struggling with how to respond, is ... that what happened in Ferguson was, in some ways unique, and in some ways not unique at all. Some people were looking to me because of what I'd been through in Ferguson. What I knew was that we needed to follow the young leadership right here in Pasadena, and it was people like Jasmine Richards and Andre Henry and Janelle Austin. It was trusting that leadership, which was really easy to do because they are extraordinary people. But I kept remembering something that Tef Poe said when he was on a panel while Ferguson was going on, and someone asked him "So what's next?" And he said, "This didn't come with no brochure." And I repeated that a lot. This doesn't come with a brochure. It is about being faithful and courageous, and it's about centering the voices that are most impacted, that have been marginalized and oppressed. And it's about trusting that leadership.

I'm still in the process of learning and reflecting from the Ferguson experience, and it continues to shape me in so many ways. There is not a day that has gone by since August 9 that I have not thought of Mike Brown and Ferguson, Alexis [Templeton], and Brittany [Ferrell]. It is such a part of who I am, and I know that I have to be part of this movement for the rest of my life. Before Ferguson happened, I was not aware of the scope of the psychological, traumatic toll of just being Black in America, the toll of exhaustion for so many who have been leaders in this movement. When I think about the number of people who have died—oh my God—Bassem was thirty-one years old and died of a heart attack. You can't tell me that wasn't related to Ferguson.

Rev. Kinman raises a critical point about the physical impact of Ferguson and the death of activist Bassem Masri who died at such a young age of a heart attack. Rev. Carlton Lee, the founder of the Flood Church in Ferguson and whom I had the privilege of interviewing for *Ferguson and Faith*, died of an apparent heart attack on June 13, 2017. However, there were several activists in the movement for Black lives that died in St. Louis and around the country under highly suspicious circumstances. This troubling fact causes a high level of suspicion about the actual perpetrators of these murders.

"Movements of church are being reborn on the streets"

Rev. Kinman continues with a theological reflection about the activist work and its connection to religious life:

> I'm a rector of a large Episcopal church. There are a lot of people who will listen to me, and I have to use that platform to make sure that I am continually speaking out. But the other thing I need to do is be sure to lift up and listen to the voices of those who are too often marginalized.
>
> A model for this to me is the story of Bartimaeus in the Gospel of Mark. Jesus is on the road to Jerusalem, and he's got places to go and people to see and important stuff on his agenda. And this blind beggar cries out by the side of the road. The disciples tell him to just shut the hell up and [that] Jesus doesn't want anything to do with him.
>
> But Jesus stops dead in his track and brings Bartimaeus to him. Bartimaeus throws of his cloak, and he's naked. He is fully who he is. Jesus brings him to the center of the community and says "What would you have me to do for you?" He brings the person who was most marginalized to the center of the community and lets him set the agenda for the whole community. Jesus stopped everything to tend to his concern.
>
> And that's the only way that Bartimaeus becomes part of the community heading towards Jerusalem—when we center that voice that has been most marginalized and oppressed and let them set the agenda for the entire community. This is what people of privilege like me need to do, and [what]

I need to keep doing better—looking for these different voices that are marginalized and not just centering and listening to them, but supporting as they reclaim the power that is rightfully theirs to set the agenda for the whole community.

Last year at All Saints Church, we did things like that during the six weeks of Advent. We had nothing but women of color in the pulpit for six weeks. We have white men in the pulpit all the time for six straight weeks but nobody notices. They noticed this, and for some, it caused discomfort. During Epiphany we had a Season of Wisdom and Revelation, and then during Lent we had gatherings and said, "Ok, tell us what you've heard?" Has that changed anything? It's hard to say but we need to continually be about those voices, and it's not just Black voices, it's brown voices, trans voices, and non-binary voices. How are we as the church continually doing this work as Jesus did with Bartimaeus of centering those voices? There [are] three things I've become more convicted about. First of all, the need for trauma-informed care. Second is—as Sekou said[— to] "Go get your cousins." And the third piece is as I have power, position, authority, and privilege, using that to center these voices that are on the margins and to direct attention there.

We took our youth choir on a civil rights pilgrimage through the South in June. We went to the 16th St. Baptist Church in Birmingham, then to Selma, New Orleans, Memphis, and ended at Canfield in Ferguson and met with Kayla Reed and Alexis Templeton. One of the most powerful things for me was taking this group of kids that I love from All Saints Church and having them meet Kayla and Alexis. Part of what I recognized was there is a sense of family that happened in Ferguson, and I will never love a group of people in the same way. And that has changed me. It has been one of the biggest blessings of my life to get to love people that much. It has caused me to view the Incarnation in a whole other way.

The first piece of it is the nature of what the young activists were expressing. It was raw and there was no pretense. Everything was stripped away and the rawness of our humanity lay bare, and it was powerful and beautiful and heartbreaking. It was all of the things that humanity is—the very essence of humanity. And for whatever reason, they welcomed me into it having every reason not to trust me. They were willing to give me an opportunity to entire into that with them. This is what has caused me to view the Body of Christ and the Incarnation in an entirely different way. There is nothing more powerful than being invited to meet people in the rawness of their humanity and vulnerability, and be invited to be that vulnerable yourself and to stand together in that brokenness.

I think about places where I've experienced that before like the Magdalene community in Thistle Farms with Rebecca Stevens and the friendship we've developed. I've been invited into that community of women in Nashville and St. Louis where they have shared their amazing life stories with me and invited me to do the same. The combination of Magdalene, Thistle Farms, and Ferguson has showed me what the church is supposed to be. That is a huge blessing, yet it also makes things harder because I can't bring myself to settle for less. And particularly the white church because our wealth and privilege have convinced us of our own self-sufficiency and we have so many walls that we build up around our hearts and each other. We fall so short of that, and it's to our own poverty.

I'm learning that part of our role in pastoring people is to care more about them than what they can offer us. That can be their [financial] pledge. That can be their respectability. That can be the invitation. That can be whatever. And part of it is I have to be really clear that I need to love the people more than anything, so I need to be willing not just to speak my truth but also to listen to the truth that is coming from them. I can't assume that I have all the answers because I am so far from that. So that's the first piece. Another thing I have experienced is a direct correlation between the amount of wealth in a community and the strength of its operative theology of scarcity. The communities that have the most wealth have the greatest theology of scarcity. The communities that I've been in that have the least material wealth have the greatest theology of abundance. Too often, when we have a lot of wealth, we think it's all about us and we think we have to defend the wealth. Otherwise, it will go away. We don't realize ourselves as living in God's hands. The time I spent in South Sudan was the most generous experience of my life and people knew that everything could be taken away. Their lives were constantly at risk. They had nothing, and they gave everything they had. And this is not to glorify poverty, but it was amazing.

I have often experienced in communities of privilege a deep sense of unworthiness and unlovability that gets masked by our privilege and power. And we build up these outward senses of our own power because, inside, we are so deeply, deeply worried that we're unlovable. I'll say this for myself, and I'm a part of this too. When I'm confronted with something like my own racism, it is easy for me to go to that place where I am ashamed and I'm like "Oh, I'm bad, and I'm unlovable." It becomes easy for me to lash out and, because of my privilege, I can shut down the conversation because I don't want to feel that way. The most common thing people will say when confronted is, "Why are you making me feel bad about being white?" And my response is "I'm not making you feel bad about being white. You've got something going on inside you. Let's talk about what that is." Transformation does not happen in the shame place. I can't make it comfortable for you, and I can't make it comfortable for me, but we need to be grounded in our own worth and lovability that doesn't come from what we own, our position, our power or the color of our skin. It comes from the fact that we're made in God's image. We've got to keep bringing ourselves to that center, and then we can venture out. We haven't done this because of our power and privilege. It's like going to the gym for the first time at fifty years old. You have not exercised those muscles and so it hurts like hell and you're like, "Oh, man, I'm never going back to that gym again." And yet you have to if you're going to change.

All Saints Church is a wonderful congregation, and I think it's easier for us to deal with things intellectually. There have been aha moments and pushback moments, but one of the biggest ahas happened outside of the church. After JR

Thomas was killed by a Pasadena police officer, a young man named Andre Henry, who is a graduate of Fuller Theological Seminary, started something with a couple of other Fuller grads called "Subversive Liturgy." We would gather on Thursday nights in front of the Pasadena Police Department and have a liturgy of lament, and we kept a memorial up for JR Thomas daily in front of the police department for a full year. And the community gathered around that, and it was a really diverse community. And that's the most transformation I've seen. It was that commitment for an entire year to gather every week and just lament. Lament our brokenness. Lament the murder of JR Thomas. Lament for his children who will not have their father. It was a community lament of asking God to hear our prayer and asking the police department to hear our cry. And that's where I saw change. I felt changed by that, and it was through that long, slow work. That was a co-journeying.

Jasmine Richards, who is the head of Black Lives Matter Pasadena, is amazing. She runs a Freedom School in summer for neighborhood kids, and a genuine sense of community building and empowerment happens there. I think there is a real limit to how much we're going to be transformed sitting in our own church, no matter how good the preaching or teaching. My own transformation only began—and it is nowhere near done—when I got out of the church and met Jesus on the street. God's out there forming church everywhere. Movements of church are being reborn on the streets.

Rev. Traci Blackmon picks up on the theme of the rebirthing of church and its implications for our collective work:

Spiritually, I think what we are seeing is a rebirthing of what it means to be church, and people are no longer accepting that church has to be a certain way. It's a different kind of spiritual awakening. It may not look like that to a lot of people. A lot of people are lamenting what they see as death, but I see it as a different kind of spiritual awakening that says God is bigger than the things that we have put God in, just as people are bigger than the things we have put them in. And as people have recognized their own power, they recognize more supreme power. And it manifests in different ways. In St. Louis, I've been watching people who feel disconnected from institutionalized church forming their own spiritual oasis and not calling it church. They're not calling it church intentionally, but they are doing some of the practices of the church. They bring together fellowship and are constructing gathering places where people of like spirit and mind can come together. They're looking at the Bible differently and putting it in conversation with other texts they hold dear in ways that help answer some of their questions. That is the concept of church no matter what you call it. *It's just being born a different way.*

I think what's next for congregations often depends on what you're setting is. If you're in a multi-racialized identity setting, that next is different than if you are in a church with people of brown skin. The difference I'm making is we have been, for some years now, trying to do diversity trainings and racial awareness in multiple group settings. And I have become convinced that we need to back away from that because we missed a step, and the step that I think is missing is how to have difficult conversations, period. We haven't done the work to have difficult conversations with one another, and somehow, we think we can come and have those conversations with honesty and integrity. And we can't. They are not transformative conversations because we haven't learned how to have difficult conversations and stay in the room with one another. That's been my personal experience, and until we learn how to create a space in which to have difficult conversations and stay in the room with one another, the conversations [will be] superficial. And that's why they don't take. That's why we keep doing them over and over again, and I think that has to precede the racialized work.

Gregory Ellison has done some wonderful work around difficult dialogue, and I think that kind of work needs to be explored.[62] I've also been thinking about the metaphor

[62] Gregory C. Ellison, Fearless Dialogues: *A New Movement for Justice* (Louisville, KY: Westminster John Knox Press, 2017).

that is used in scripture of the body being one but made of many parts because I think that we are so overwhelmed with issues and concerns of today—and they're all valid— that we take on so much that we're not effective at much. I wonder what might happen if churches [were to begin] to do some type of communal assessment and say, "This is who we are, and this is what we want to be known for, and this is our contribution to the body." In other words, we're not the whole body in the scheme of the connection of churches regionally or nationally or globally. We are an arm of it. Churches don't tend to, in my opinion, think of themselves like that. They think of themselves as a body and their members are pieces of the body, and that's true.

But, when you connect churches together, then how do we figure out what part of the body we are as churches and do that part of the body well versus being so crisis oriented.

We're also going to have to respond to crisis, but there are particular parts of the body, in terms of whole churches, that are uniquely suited for things that other parts of the body are not suited for. How do we strengthen those pieces of the body that are uniquely crafted to have impact in certain areas? For example, if we look around our region, how do we identify churches that can actually have strong mentoring programs that reach beyond their walls that would really work well? How do we identify them and support that work in those congregations? How do we identify the congregations that could have effective unhoused ministries and have the facilities and people to open up shelter-type facilities? How do we support that part of the body doing that work? All of this requires churches to ask "And what is my part of the body?" It requires a collaboration that churches don't have even within denominations and certainly within neighborhoods. Too many churches have competitive mentalities rather than collaborative mentalities. It's one of the reasons, I think, we were not even more impactful during Ferguson as church units because we have a competitive spirit versus a collaborative spirit. Too often it became about who is leading and who is getting attention, press conferences, and accolades, rather than who is being served by our collective efforts.

Rev. Shaun Jones is a native of St. Louis and was active in the Ferguson movement. He now lives in New York and is the pastor of Star of Bethlehem Baptist Church. He recounts his experience of engaging his congregation in addressing issues of systemic racial injustice in their Community:

> I pastor a church in a village called Ossining in New York [State]. The church's name is Star of Bethlehem Baptist Church and it [was founded in 1890]. After our first interview, I became a community organizer officially through Metropolitan Congregations United (MCU), which was on the ground with many other organizations during the Ferguson uprising. I was able to actually get trained as a community organizer, and it has been a blessing for me. Now I get to use both skill sets of pastoral leadership and community organizing in the work that I do here in Ossining.
>
> Prior to the Ferguson uprising I'd worked with the Clergy Coalition of St. Louis as an organizer to try and gather people together for justice-focused endeavors that were happening around the state or in St. Louis. But it was through the work done in Ferguson that I became affiliated with MCU, which is part of the Gamaliel National Network, and they were investing in faith leaders such as myself. Part of my work was trying to bridge the gap between MCU, which was more of a white organization that became multicultural, and the Clergy Coalition of St. Louis, which was a predominately Black group. I was to try and be the bridge between the two to try and work together cohesively within the St. Louis metropolitan area.
>
> It's important for pastors to have a theology that is grounded in justice and addresses the turmoil that we see on the news or in our lives. People come to church and they are looking for some perspective from God. What is God saying about this? Does God care? We say God cares. In the Black church we say, "He sits high and looks low." But what does

that mean when the world I live in is mean and I'm being discriminated against at work because of my race, gender, or socioeconomic status? And where do I get encouragement but also guidance and instruction for how to deal with this?

There is no doubt that pastors and preachers have an influential role in helping congregations think critically about troubling societal norms or personal experiences, and offer a theological reflection on how God's presence/activity is understood in the midst of it. Rev. Dr. Frank Thomas, Professor of Homiletics at Christian Theological Seminary, has written extensively on the role of preaching in the African American experience. In his book *How to Preach a Dangerous Sermon*, Dr. Thomas details a homiletical method that equips preachers with a framework for responding to challenging socio-political issues of our time with a call to action that is shaped by a moral vision that promotes equality and care for all:

The ability of the preacher, intuitive or otherwise, in the midst of the chaotic experiences of life and existence, to grasp and share God's abiding wisdom and ethical truth in order to benefit the individual and common humanity. Moral imagination of the true Christian faith advocates against racism, misogyny, homophobia, discrimination, cynicism, scapegoating, blame, and so on, and visions all human beings created in the image of God, and as such, warrants the ritual and benefits of freedom for all.[63]

Dr. Thomas cites this type of preaching as dangerous because it challenges the status quo and can inspire the hearer to work to build the kind of society that truly fosters liberty and justice for all.

Rev. Shaun Jones shares some of the resistance work that he has led his congregation to do in New York:

And so for me at Star of Bethlehem, I realize that I am the pastor of the largest Black church in my community, and the African American population continues to decline in our town. At one point were 24, 25 percent of the population.

---

[63] Frank A. Thomas, *How to Preach a Dangerous Sermon* (Nashville, TN: Abingdon Press, 2018), xl.

We are not about 16 percent. Many African Americans are being priced out of the town. Too many cannot afford the rent or those who are homeowners cannot afford the taxes. So now the majority of our congregation no longer lives in the town in which they were raised. They drive in 30, 40 minutes. I have members who live in Connecticut. Lately, we have been fighting for the Emergency Tenant Protection Act (ETPA). The ETPA was a law put on the books in 1975 in New York state for the City of New York and several of its boroughs to provide rental control stabilization so people were not priced out of their apartments and their homes. Our town had never enacted the policy.

There had been many who had tried for years and so we finally got the victory after a three-year battle. Now this means a lot for Ossining because our school system is 58 percent Hispanic and we have a large Ecuadorian, Dominican, and Puerto Rican community who, along with African Americans, may not be able to afford the taxes and high rental rates. Many work as teachers' aides or CNAs and service positions. Some are teachers and [have] other similar paying jobs but they can't afford the rent and taxes.

After a three-year battle to prove there was a housing crisis, our mayor, who got re-elected by only 219 votes, is trying to get rid of this protection. When I first came to Star of Bethlehem, I took my very first Bible study class to City Hall to let the officials know that we care about the housing needs of this community. While I was looking forward to just pastoring our church and dealing with our regular Sunday morning and weekly activities, I am now fighting again with my members to try and seek justice for our community. We're fighting for many of those who are disabled or senior citizens. We've called upon our county executives and state legislators to tell our mayor, "You don't have a viable solution to help 1,500 people in this community have a fair rent and leases." There are people in the town that don't even have a lease, which is a normal protection. Sunday morning must be a training ground for me to make hell on earth become heaven for me where I live. When I moved here, I was associated with Ferguson more than St. Louis—

even though I said I was from St. Louis. People would say "Oh yeah, he's from Ferguson," and I'm like, "Yeah, I guess I am." I don't think of myself that way, but for the outside world, that has been my label, and I'm learning to adopt and accept it as it is. It's a mark. It's a badge of honor. It is also a moment of trauma for many of us whether you were on the streets or just living in the city as it was going on every day. I take it and say "Hey, it'll be my cross to bear."

Brittini Gray pushes back against the current contours of the church and challenges it to transform into a more liberative space if it is to continue:

I think that the church—Black or mainline—is too representative of the status quo, and for that to change I think we have to let church die in the ways in which we currently conceptualize it. Having worked with a lot of white congregations through my professional career, having engaged with Black congregations on many levels of my own life, I see the conversations that churches are having, and I just don't believe that there's enough transformation in that space for those conversations to also be reflected in the preaching, to also be reflected in the teaching, since churches serve as a space where our world views are shaped. I don't see enough truth telling taking place for a racial healing to really take root in people's lives. When you talked to me for *Ferguson and Faith*, I was still very much trying to hold on to the ideas of what church communities were supposed to be. And, since then, I've given [that] up.

So I would say that's a norm for people in my generation in just seeing the contradictions that exist with the church, all the ways in which many churches are not safe spaces for people and their full identities and their world views. I think people are beyond the point where the institutional significance of the church is worth investing in at the expense of yourself. And that's not to say that Millennials are not very spiritually based and hold a higher value system, but the disconnect between the institution and what people's spiritual journeys look like is real.

I really do believe that how we do conceptualize church has to be eradicated and a new vision of what church can be has to emerge. In a lot of ways, this is more biblical [*laughs*] than what we currently have. That is how the first church was formed—out of needing a radical difference from the religious institutions' status quo—and I feel like that's where we are now. One of the things that movement space has provided is a return to indigenous and traditional practices. I think that there is a yearning for that in religious spaces for people. One that incorporates different ideologies than what we have come to sternly understand church as being. I think that there is a recognition that some of the old traditions have held and provided spaces for people to survive. I think of traditions like an honoring of the ancestors or even the use of sage. Six years ago, most of the people I know would have been like "Hmm. That's some voodoo stuff. Why are you messing with that? Leave it alone." And now it's super commonplace for folks to use herbs as part of their spiritual practice. It's believed that herbs can shift the energy and cleanse a space of whatever spirits may have been [there]. Things that have been literally demonized in Christianity [are] coming back to the forefront for people as a valuable practice. And science even supports that certain herbs actually [affect] our brain cells. There is value in connecting pieces that [have] previously been disconnected from people and seeing wholeness in that connection.

When we talk about honoring the ancestors, I remember growing up in Chicago. I had a very pro-Black upbringing, and I had a very Christian upbringing, but those two things were like completely separate for me. And [when] the focus was on Mary and David and Jesus but [there was] no remembrance of who your great-grandmother was, what does that do in terms of the memory that the body holds for people trying to connect to healing in themselves? So that's an example of what I mean when I say we need a return to old traditions that bring connection back into spiritual practices as being important.

I interpret the space of church to really be a supporter of state and how values get reinforced in the church, especially and particularly in Black church spaces. There is still a focus on middle-class aspirations for Black people that have not [laughs] proven to be successful or true for the masses. It may be true for some people, but it is not true for the masses. That premise has to be done away with. The church has to get out of bed with the state because you can't hold place for people to feel safe and to be transformed while also putting restrictions and limiting their self-expression or their full identity. I think that there are like huge ideological shifts, practices, and doctrine that have to be redone in ways that are no longer oppressive and exploitive because I think that a lot of churches are able to benefit, for example, off of the labor of Black women. So it serves them well to have these conflicting messages about sex and about who's the head of the household or whatever [laughs] stereotypical subject you want to bring up. It serves the church well to have those in place for their maintenance.

I'm not sure that they knew what they were asking for, but I went to a very established Baptist church earlier this year to talk about abundant living. And I did not talk about it traditionally in the ways that I have heard it talked about growing up Baptist, but I talked about what did it mean— because it was a roomful of women—what did it mean for us to take care of ourselves first as a way to live abundantly, like to actually care for ourselves. And, in that space, I had an eighty-year-old women who was said, "You know, I've been taking care of these kids, and I've been at the church every Sunday. I'm going to take a Sunday for me!" Someone else said, "I've been single for twenty years because I've been saying that Jesus is my husband, but I'm going to get on these dating sites, but I need y'all to help me." Everything shifted by the end of the ninety-minute session because, when I came into the room, they weren't trying to have none of that. But by the end of the time, they were really able to imagine, "You know, I think I'm with this self-care of myself." I prefer the word imagine over reform and all of these other things. I really do think it is about our imagination, the space of intuitive, honest, authentic, creativity in tune with the

Creator. These are the spaces where we are able to envision something other than what is.

Rev. Jacque Foster is the pastor of Compton Heights Christian Church in St. Louis. That congregation provided safe sanctuary support for protestors and organizers during the Ferguson uprising, and they have continued in the movement for racial justice. She reflects on the implications of that experience:

I don't think there's been a return to normal. I don't know what normal would be. Normal, I suppose, was some denial that the problem of racial hatred and violence was a pervasive as it is. I don't believe we have returned to that as normal, and I don't believe we can. Soon after our church had served as sanctuary space and safe space during the Ferguson uprising, one of our elders asked, "How do we continue to be safe space, a sanctuary space?" There was a sense that this isn't going away so we moved forward with it. And what I've seen is that more people in the congregation are active politically and socially. People in the congregation who would never have thought they needed to be down at City Hall and taking any kind of action were saying, "Well, that's where we are now, and I guess it's where I need to be."

One of the changes I have seen has to do with some of what has happened since this current president [Trump] was running and elected. While we are still focusing on racism, we also see the attacks of people in the LGBTQ community and women. In our conversations now, we talk about intersectionality and raise awareness about how all of these issues come together. It's hard to separate at this point.

I was on sabbatical last summer, and when I came back, what I found was what a pastor always wants to find—that the congregation has gone right on doing what they are called to do. Our elders were studying the book *Prophetic Lament* by Soong-Chan Rah, and the congregation had restarted a book study group that had ended with their study of *Just*

Mercy by Bryan Stevenson looking at the issues of mass incarceration. So what I saw was a congregation that has awakened, and that on its own has moved in directions of educating and working for justice.

Part of the lament and grief is that we are in a time when bold white supremacy has a strong, strong following. And that's terrifying. It's calling us to double down on the Gospel, to be clear about naming what is happening in our midst. We can't lament if we don't name it. We can't heal if we don't name it. There are times when I've talked about these issues again and again and again, and I think to myself, "Can I go in the pulpit one more Sunday and talk about that? Am I just bringing us down?" So I try to find that balance and talk about what's happening in a way that is life-giving, in a way that promises fullness of life for everyone. That's what the season of Advent is about. When we say, in the midst of our injustice, come. In the midst of our pain, come and make us a people who live out the presence of Jesus the Christ. This call reminds us to remain aware and be present in the fight for justice.

My husband and I, like many people I know, have reached a point where when we see the police pull someone over, we go around the block and come back around and even park there at times, nearby. We do this because we don't trust what the police are going to do when they pull over a person of color, and we have to be present. But that's not enough. We have to continue to do the work to bring our police to accountability. Here in St. Louis there was a move to put together the Civilian Oversight Board, but that board has no power. It's controlled by the police department. So in our cities where that kind of abusive control by the police is held at this level, we have to continue to work to call for accountability. And when the entire political system is protecting that model, it's a slow, slow process. But we cannot give up.

When we talk about God's reign, it's in the midst of the worst of times that scripture tells us that we see it coming. We see signs, and the signs don't look good. But I have to believe that the realm of God, where people live together in peace and justice, is coming. So we live in the already and the not yet. It's important that we live as if the realm is here because it has already been given to us. We've already been made one but we've just haven't recognized it yet. We haven't lived into it yet, but it feels like it comes closer every time and in every way when we live as if it is.

Living into the hope

Jia Lian Yang is an Eden Seminary graduate who was named in *Ferguson and Faith* as Karen Yang. She is currently the co-host/lead producer of We Live Here, a podcast produced by St. Louis Public Radio and PRX. She describes aspects of her vocational and personal journey, to include being identified by her Chinese name, Jia Lian:

> Soon after I graduated from seminary, I started a full-time job working as a family minister at Metropolitan Community Church of Greater St. Louis. It's an LGBT-led and affirming church, and I worked there for about nine months. After that, I did several community-based types of work that supported Solidarity Economy St. Louis, which is a network of individuals and groups working for an economy that is based on cooperation rather than exploitation.[64] I supported Latinos en Axion in St. Louis in putting on their kind of Mexican Independence Day festival. Then I worked for a consultant who did marketing, branding, and community outreach for different organizations, and I was primarily working with Green Rivers Greenway.
>
> During that time, it was a kind of existential too, because who are you if you don't have a full-time vocation? In seminary, you're taught it's a very straightforward path, but I was pursuing a dual degree of social work and divinity, so I really had to work to find my way. Ultimately what I ended up doing in that in-between space was I started a podcast called *Who Raised You?* with Treasure Shields Redmond, who is a poet. Her father, Eugene Redmond, is Poet Laureate of East St. Louis. She is also a former professor of English

---

[64] "Solidarity Economy St. Louis," Solidarity Economy St. Louis, June 1, 2020, http://www.solidaritystl.org/.

and helps college-bound teens and their parents get their children through college for no debt or low debt. We started this podcast because I really wanted to record stories similar to *Ferguson and Faith*. I wanted to record the stories of incredible people around me.

After the Ferguson uprising, people were much more mobilized to take direct action, but they were also much more interested in forming organizations, collectives, or their own initiatives, such as an entrepreneur-based business or healing retreat centers. People were starting to do creative things that formed the infrastructure for resistance and experiences and services that help to make for a better world. So I was seeing incredible people around me doing these things while also out in the streets, for example, when the Stockley verdict came down.

So the very same people who are creating art, music, healing spaces, and services like therapy for folks of color, they're the same people on the streets. And so I noticed that we were moving very fast, and if one day you're out in the streets, and another day you're busy creating things, you may not slow down to actually tell the stories of how you got there or what's going on. I just had a lot of love for people, people who became my friends who I may have met in direct action or just know that we have the same values in the community. And I wanted to record those stories.

This may sound really strange, but I think when you're on the streets protesting, people do that out of hope that things will change. But, at the same time, I think there's also a sense that people get used to kind of pain and trauma and suffering. And I think it sometimes surprises people that we can win. Even if we can't, like, I believe that we will win!

People have incredible faith in each other and the ability of community to mobilize and particularly of Black women to lead struggle and also to be brilliant. We are seeing organized efforts across the county. Wherever there is oppression, there is resistance throughout history. And so it's kind of building and the creativity and brilliance that folks have—particularly Black folks, particularly Black women, particularly queer Black women—they've been learning and building [on] what their ancestors have made. And we are seeing some of the fruits of that now.

What surprised me is the ability of people to organize and win. I think I knew that that was possible, but I didn't know what it looked like. When you're resisting and hoping for things to get better, so much of the criticism you get is, "Well, this is the way that things are for these reasons." How's that possible? Organizers are not only gathering people together based on values, but they also have the data to say, for example, if we weren't spending money to support a Workhouse jail, it could be diverted to social services. We could have community participatory budgeting meetings to allocate resources. We don't actually have to live this way. So when we're saying abolish jails, abolish prisons, abolish police, there are folks who can actually envision the way forward, and we can actually see like a small sliver of what that future looks like.

It's a question of "Do people see themselves in this vision of the future?" If people feel like their current position or privilege is going to be threatened by gains or well-being of people who are marginalized, they're going to resist that because they can't envision a way that they can [still] get what *they* need. Or they're afraid that, by putting forth a more imaginative vision, the current status quo of good enough for them will be taken away.

For me and also for people who understand what's actually involved in these imaginative visions for well-being, *radical* is not necessarily a bad word. Charlene Carruthers of the Black Youth Project 100 (BYP100) says that their organization was formed in the Black radical tradition when they're adopting the Combahee River Collective and Black Panther Party kind of principles. That's the Black radical tradition. It is not a bad thing. What *is* a bad thing is racism, white supremacy masquerading as the so-called "alt-right."

Jia Lian means beautiful lotus, and it's the Chinese name my mom gave me along with Karen, which is my government name. When I was growing up, I thought it was a kind of shallow name [*laughs*] because I didn't think surface beauty is important. But, now, I've been reflecting a lot on what lotuses mean in lots of different cultures, and it's a flower that blooms and grows in mud. That's why it is spiritually significant for a lot of people. I started going by Jia Lian mostly because I realized there are lot of Karen Yangs out there. [*laughs*] And, as I was doing the creative work of the podcast, I wanted people to be able to associate my name with the podcast. I started realizing that, when people call me Jia Lian and pronounce it correctly, I feel this emotional response, partly because I'm working with artists now, and artists just have all sorts of names. I thought to myself, if artists can go by whatever the name they want, so can I.

And I found that people who take the time to know how to pronounce and say it, they're actually taking the time to get to know me. What's also kind of funny is, the more white people are calling the cops on Black folks, the more old white names they're using as nicknames. For instance, there was Barbeque Becky who called the police on a group of Black people barbequing in a park. Now there are memes about "No one asked you to ruin the potato salad, Karen." So whenever I see that I'm like "Oh, my gosh." I don't think I can go back to Karen.

In her reflection below, Brittini Gray asks the poignant question, "How do we cultivate joy intentionally in this space of social and political pain?" Finding joy is an intentional act of resistance. Seeking out one's purpose in the midst of pain is a radical act of self-love. Reaching out to others and building relationships, camaraderie, and mutual support can provide a sustaining balm through the difficult time. Brittini continues her reflections on how she tapped into her artistic and creative gifts as a source and expression of her joy:

The impact of Ferguson for me has been really homing in on my own analysis, getting sharper about how I critique systems, how I understand our relationship to them. I think it transformed me personally in that I already had discomfort with the status quo. I think that Ferguson pushed me completely into the zone of being okay with operating outside of the status quo. And so, for me, that has looked like leaving my job which I was with when Ferguson first happened, leaving the church, graduating but really doing away with institutional spaces because I was feeling as though they were oppressive to my own well-being. So being mindful of not only ... how we are impacted societally but what's the impact on my personal health and well-being. And so becoming much more intentional about that, relieving my own stress and trauma through healing practices. I went through somatics, started getting more intentional about how I used my art as an avenue for healing, and then just creating spaces that really bridged what I think is crucial for the liberation of people, which is community space, which is organizing the expression and creativity that art brings, as well as being very intentional about having spaces for people to heal. And so now I find myself fully living into that.

I have a documentary that has been in three film festivals now called *Movement Women: The Making of a CREW*. It focuses on women in the movement and all women from St. Louis who have been in my circle somehow. And what I find interesting is [that] some people who see the documentary ask "Well, why is it only women?" And the reality is, when you were out there and even now today, it's mainly women who are doing the work of liberation even though we still continue to see, societally, emphasis placed on how men are impacted. Women are impacted too. It's women that are doing the work. And so really bringing a light to the stories of women in this work has been important for me. Originally, it began as, like, "OK, we're coming up on the three-year anniversary. How do we just create space to reflect on our and where we are today?" Originally, I just wanted to do that as a kind of raw collection, hit the record button. But it evolved. We were open to the creative process and the vision of Aziza, my co-director and co-producer, and wanting to see this represented as a short film. So that's been one piece of my art.

The other piece has been poetry, as I've been a poet for twenty years now and kind of a spoken word artist for the past six or seven years. I used to always think of art very traditionally. And so, if I didn't paint or play an instrument, I didn't really see myself as an artist, and because a lot of my poetry was personal, just how I processed my own trauma as a young girl, I didn't really assume that title until I started actually performing my own art. So I would still perform poetry, but I would read a piece from Maya Angelou or something from Tupac.

About six or seven years ago I started using it in my organizing and in my public speaking as a way to kind of calm my nerves. Before I would give a talk, I would do a poem to warm me up. My concept of myself as an artist became much more defined after Ferguson.

Now it has drawn me into new relationships with people like Dr. Robyn Henderson Espinoza. We're collaborating on a project called *Activist Theology*, in which Robyn is writing the kind of narrative prose pieces of it, and I've written poetry for the book.[65] And then I hold a space here with two other poets, Sunni Hutton and Treasure Shields Redmond, on poetry and politics. I also plan to launch a zine, which is an independently published magazine that's at the intersection of art and healing. We've had eighteen artists submit work for it that answers the prompt, "How do we cultivate joy intentionally in this space of social and political pain?"

Brittini's deeper dive into her artistic creativity has created multiple opportunities for her to find joy in the midst of the pain, and she is not alone. Movements of resistance have often found ways to weave in artistic expressions as a way of reinforcing and strengthening resolve and keeping participants grounded in their purpose in the midst of the pain. Beating the drums, chanting slogans such as "No Justice, No Peace!," and singing freedom songs has been integral to keeping the spirits of people lifted in the face of seemingly insurmountable hardship. Although there is nothing "joyous" about the devastating impact of systemic racial inequity and its effect on Black people's live, cultivating joy in the midst of it is its own form of resistance to the oppression and devaluing of Black lives.

One of the most well-known artistic expressions that brought a tremendous amount of joy and pride in the midst of the challenges of advocating for Black lives was the release of the Marvel comic-turned-

---

[65] Robyn Henderson-Espinoza, *Activist Theology* (Minneapolis, MN: Fortress Press, 2019).

movie, *The Black Panther.* Released in January 2018, Black people went to the movies in droves to see this cinematic depiction of a vibrant, colorful, soulful, and purposeful fictitious country in Africa called Wakanda. In Wakanda, Black people designed, innovated, inspired, protected, and cultivated their own way of life and culture and managed some of the world's most valuable resources. And it was beautiful! They scenery, costumes, and actors, including the late Chadwick Boseman who played King T'Challa, were remarkable, and I distinctly remember leaving the movie feeling so hopeful and inspired that I too crossed my arms over my chest and shouted "Wakanda Forever!" Even Delta Airlines got in on the action by designating the destination on the board of an empty Atlanta airline gate "Wakanda." The thrill of the psychological and emotional impact *The Black Panther* was a wonder to behold.

Music and rhythm remained an integral part of protests.
KB Frazier is leading with the jembe drum on the way to
police headquarters. *(Photo by David Gerth)*

A delegation of faith leaders from the United States was invited to give testimony at a hearing at the World Council of Churches in Geneva, Switzerland, in September 2017. The initial focus of the hearing was to include issue of racism and discrimination in various countries; however, once the Charlottesville tiki torch night ride made international headlines, they chose to focus only on the issue of racism in the United States. The title of the hearing was International Ecumenical Hearing on Racism, Discrimination, Afrophobia, and Xenophobia: The Experience of People of African Descent in the USA.

Building a World We Want to See

Dr. Leah Gunning Francis, Rev. Traci Blackmon,
Bishop Mary Ann Swenson, Dr. Iva Carruthers, Rev. Mike Kinmon,
and Rev. Karen Georgia Thompson at the World Council of Churches
in Geneva, Switzerland. *(Photo courtesy of Segma Asfaw)*

The delegation from the United States. *(Photo courtesy of Segma Asfaw)*

SENSORY WORK

Finding joy in the midst of difficulty can require a tremendous amount of emotional and physical energy. I invite you to read Maya Angelou's poem slowly, and "step" inside of it and try on her words. You can view the poem here: https://www.youtube.com/watch?v=JqOqo50LSZ0

- What is the energy you feel?
- What images come to mind?
- Do you recall a time when you had to find strength to overcome a difficult situation?
- How did you do it?

I encourage you to consider the parents and loved ones people who have died as a result of police violence. Although we may not be able to "walk" their shoes, we can empathize with how difficult their journey must be.

- What might it look and feel like to embark on a journey toward racial equality with them in mind?
- How do might we image racial justice as an expression of joy?

* * *

The Lord works righteousness and justice for all the oppressed. —
Psalm 103:6

CHAPTER 7

·······················

Reclaiming Our Time

In May 2017, Congresswoman Maxine Waters of California sent a letter to US Treasury Secretary Steven Mnuchin to inquire about the president's financial ties to Russia. During a House Financial Services Committee Meeting in July, Waters asked Mnuchin why he had not responded to her letter. During a hearing, each committee member is only allotted a certain amount of time to ask their questions. Mnuchin knew the rules and chose to use his response time to lavish Congressman Waters with faux compliments instead of answering her question about the letter. As soon as she realized the deflection game Mnuchin was playing, she started hammering her gavel and said, "Reclaiming my time. Reclaiming my time."

What might it mean for us to "reclaim our time" in the years ahead? Reclaiming our time is a critical first step to: 1) redeeming the time we have lost as a country by traveling roads paved with white supremacy, 2) redirecting our efforts toward charting new pathways for racial justice and equity to flourish, and 3) rewriting our narrative to proclaim that the way things are, is not the way things have to be. All lives will not matter until Black lives matter. No more calls for peace without justice, for unity without repairing the damage that has been done, or for civility without accountability. Reclaiming our time means not getting distracted and sidetracked by efforts that are simply meant to take us of the course of racial justice. We can take a cue of courage from Congresswoman Waters and be willing to say "No. I am not going to sit here and waste my time while you launch an effort of mass distraction by not addressing the issue at hand." Reclaiming my time!

As we work to "reclaim our time" and chart a racially just pathway forward, we must do at least three things: keep talking about racism and white supremacy; move from being an ally to an accomplice; and remember that real lives are at stake. Rev. Shaun Jones, pastor of Star of Bethlehem Baptist Church in Ossining, New York, shares a stark reminder about the roads that have been paved with white supremacy:

Our country was built on racism from chattel slavery. The infrastructure, the economy, the actual physical buildings were built on the backs of enslaved people. And because our country has yet to honestly acknowledge and repent and make penance for those actions, I don't believe that we can move forward. One of the things you hear in a twelve-step program is that you have to admit there is a problem. And, for a long time, people felt like calling us rabble rousers for disrupting the flow of commerce. But we were trying to make the point that we have a problem. If all lives mattered, then you wouldn't have to say that black lives matter, but because ... our communities are over-policed and infected with structural and economic disparities, we have to say "black lives matter" because we want to encourage Black people to believe that we have value and we matter.

And we also want to speak to the powers that be and say, "We're not going to stand for this anymore, and we're going to tear down injustice and rebuild a new system that values to belong in the American Dream." We're redoing the dream because the dream that was manifest was based on occupying other people's land and taking from them. We're changing the value system to say it's not about conquering but about how we can have a shared community, a beloved community that Dr. King and others have spoken so eloquently about.

Redoing the dream and charting a racially just path forward requires us to tell the truth about this country's racist history and the extent of the physical, emotional, and financial damage that has been done. At the heart of the marches, rallies, highway shutdowns, boycotts, and protests is a cry for the humanity of Black people to be seen and valued. Too often, when we say "Black Lives Matter," we are met with a retort of "All Lives Matter!" This retort is intended to dismiss the claims that are being made about the ways in which Black lives are not valued in the same way as white lives. All of the national data related to health, wealth, education, housing, and criminal justice tells a story of inequity along racial lines. Instead of the phrase being widely embraced as a rallying call to eradicate these inequities, it is often used as a weapon against Black people and to charge supporters of the phrase as supporting some type of radical terrorist group. The FBI has gone so far as to make an official designation of "Black Identity Extremists" as an organization that does not actually exist. The report prepared by the FBI Counter Terrorism Division in 2017 to make this designation is widely seen as the latest racist scare tactic to dissuade people from protesting against police violence.[66]

We cannot neglect the truth about policing and the fact that we have never had an anti-racist model of policing in the United States. In an article for the New Yorker magazine, Dr. Jill Lepore, a professor of history at Harvard University, shows the contours of how slavery was a progenitor for the burgeoning business of policing that we have today.[67] We have to tell the truth and construct pathways that will lead us down a pathway where Black parents no longer have to give "the talk" to their children about what to do when they encounter the police or watch video after video of an unarmed Black person being killed by a police officer.

The primary rationale we hear from police officers about why they killed an unarmed Black person is that he or she felt "threatened" and "feared for her/his life." The rationale of "I felt threatened and feared for my life" leads us to a glaring omission in the discourse about and investigation into the US Capitol invasion on January 6, 2021. Why didn't the police feel threatened enough to draw their guns and threaten to shoot the people who were busting through police barricades, beating police officers with objects such as the American flag pole, and breaking out the Capitol windows? Why didn't they feel threatened enough to shoot the invaders when they breached the Capitol doors and made their way onto the House floor? Why did they show so much physical restraint to the peril of officers' safety? We need answers to these questions, and the same kind of deference shown to unarmed Black people who are too often killed *while committing no crime*. We can't keep going down this deadly road.

[66] Khaled A. Beydoun and Justin Hansford, "The F.B.I.'s Dangerous Crackdown on 'Black Identity Extremists'," The New York Times (The New York Times, November 15, 2017), https://www.nytimes.com/2017/11/15/opinion/black-identity-extremism-fbi-trump.html.

[67] Jill Lepore, "The Invention of the Police," The New Yorker, July 7, 2020, https://www.newyorker.com/magazine/2020/07/20/the-invention-of-the-police.

We must keep talking constructively about racism and white supremacy and chart a racially just pathway forward.

Moving from ally to accomplice

Several years ago I was on a panel with activist Darnell Moore, and he said something that has stuck with me to this day. He was making the point that we need white people who are serious about dismantling racial injustice to move from being allies to accomplices. That was an "aha" moment for me because the designation of "ally" seems to give people the option of opting in and out of dismantling racial injustice at will. Allies can easily take the posture of being with and for the cause when convenient. However, accomplices are often associated with a cause because they are willing to put something on the line. Accomplices are usually associated with a crime (e.g. driving a bank robber to the bank); however, we can reclaim the term for a positive purpose. Being an accomplice to racial justice and equity means that you are willing to be so identified with the cause, that you are willing to put something on the line.

Protest in Indianapolis after the killing of George Floyd
on May 31, 2020. *(Photo by Ray Mills)*

For many, they have put their bodies on the line in protest. For others, they have used their influence to speak out against racial injustice to their peers, risking being ostracized. Some have made significant investments of time and money to support the organizations that are focused on this work. The opportunities are endless. Dismantling systemic racism is ultimately white people's work to do.

Kerry Connelly, CTS MDiv student, author of Good White Racist

Christian Theological Seminary professor Dr. Rob Saler moderated a discussion with CTS students Kerry Connelly, Cassidy Hall, and Mason Mennenga on Kerry's book Good White Racist: Confronting Your Role in Racial Injustice.[68] *(Photo courtesy of Christian Theological Seminary)*

* * *

Time for Action!

"Are you awake?"

As I slowly opened one eye on this early morning with a "Who wants to know?" glare, my husband said, "I think we need to go to Georgia."

Christmas was approaching, and we'd been talking about how were going to spend our post-Christmas-in-COVID-19 break. Raphael Warnock and Jon Ossoff were in a tightly run race for the US Senate, and if they won, Democrats would gain control of the Senate with Vice President-elect Harris breaking any tied votes.

"Let me make some calls today and see what I can find out," I said before trying to catch a few more minutes sleep until the alarm clock went off.

---

[68] Kerry Connelly, *Good White Racist: Confronting Your Role in Racial Injustice* (Louisville, KY: Westminster John Knox Press, 2020).

By the next day, we had orchestrated a plan to drive to Georgia, rent a house, and canvass in north Georgia for Warnock and Ossoff. On December 26, 2020, we packed our sons, my sister, and an assortment of belongings into the van and headed south on I-65. Fortunately, the weather was sunny and traffic was moving along nicely. However, as we crossed the Tennessee state line, a feeling of dread emerged in my spirit.

"I wonder if we can see any of the damage," I thought to myself as we approached Nashville.

My mother is from Pulaski, Tennessee, a small town about an hour south of Nashville. She and my father met in college at Tennessee State University, married, and after graduation, moved back to my father's hometown of Philadelphia. By the time I was born, they'd moved across the Delaware River, and I was raised in Willingboro, New Jersey. However, my sister, brother, and I spent nearly every summer vacation at my maternal grandparent's home in Pulaski. This was our second home, and the majority of my extended family still lives in Tennessee.

My heart broke wide open after the immediate shock wore off from learning about the 2020 Christmas Day bombing in Nashville. I worried about the safety of my family, friends, and the city at large, and prayed that everyone was okay. I guess you could say that the bomber was not trying to kill anyone because he gave a fifteen minute warning before detonating the bomb that devastated an entire downtown block.[69] Nonetheless, the extensive explosion destroyed buildings and shattered people's peace of mind. What was the bomber's motivation? Was he connected to a hate group or did he truly act alone? Why now? While these and many other questions remain unanswered, what we know for sure is that the threat of acts of domestic terrorism remains.

Our van was quiet as we passed the downtown area. I noticed a faint smell of fire, but we couldn't see any damage from the highway. "Mom, I can't get a signal," said our youngest son. I looked at my phone and noticed the same thing. We later learned that the explosion had disrupted AT&T's wireless service, and we didn't regain service until we crossed the Georgia state line.

---

[69] Natalie Allison and Adam Tamburin, "Retracing the Key Moments after the Christmas Morning Bombing in Nashville," Timeline of the Christmas morning bombing in Nashville (The Tennessean, January 10, 2021), https://www.tennessean.com/in-depth/news/local/2021/01/10/timeline-christmas-morning-bombing-nashville/6578915002/.

Leah, Rodney, Evan, and Desmond campaigning
in north Georgia. (Photo by Carla Gunning)

We spent two days canvassing our assigned area in north Georgia. Masked, gloved, and armed with campaign literature, we knocked on more than one hundred doors and spread the good word about the candidates. It was a blessing for us to show our sons a tangible way to work on behalf of candidates that support policies that align with our values of human flourishing and faithful stewardship of God's creation, to "pray with our feet" as we put our faith into action in the tradition of Fannie Lou Hamer and Bob Moses, and to enable them to see themselves as active participants in the struggle for justice and equality.

Rodney, Evan, Carla, and Desmond canvassing in north Georgia. *(Photo by Leah Gunning Francis)*

We specifically requested to canvass in a predominately Black neighborhood for three reasons. First, we wanted to reduce the chance of being dubbed as "suspicious" as we walked along those residential streets and have someone call the police. There was no time, energy, or bandwidth to have to deal with that nonsense.

Second, we wanted to minimize any racially motivated conflict when we rang a doorbell. We were in north Georgia and in an area that is heavily Republican. If there was going to be conflict, we at least wanted to know that it wasn't because we are Black.

Third, people often feel more comfortable talking to others with whom they can relate. Racism was on the ballot as the Republican candidates used it as a billy club to try and beat back the truth that Warnock and Ossoff were shining a spotlight on abhorrent records of putting profit over people and personal gain over the common good. The WNBA Atlanta Dream team, which Republican candidate Kelly

Loeffler co-owns, even came out against her and threw their support behind Warnock after she publicly disparaged Black Lives Matter.[70] Seeing this team stand side by side wearing "Vote Warnock" shirts in repudiation of Loeffler's racist views was a powerful sight to behold! Since racism held a prominent place in the Georgia Senate race, we thought that Black people might feel more comfortable talking to other Black people about the hotly contested election.

And talk they did! Most people we encountered were very receptive, a few were skeptical, and a couple said they had only voted in the general election to get Trump out of office. They offered a sober reminder that people want to know how their lives will improve by voting for a particular candidate. Just voting for a person because of his or her race, gender, or religious affiliation is not a sufficient reason for many voters. People want to know what difference their vote will make for every day folks, not just the candidate's aspirations. Real lives are at stake.

The Ferguson uprising, and the many that have followed in response to police violence, have moved us a few steps along the pathway toward racial justice and equality. We cannot pretend that we have not seen the tragedies that we saw. The election of Joe Biden and Kamala Harris presents, for some, an opportunity to move further along the path of racial justice and equity. I see their election not as a guaranteed opportunity but as giving us a greater chance to implore them to do what is in the interest of racial justice and equity. It will still take work: resisting efforts/legislation incompatible with a racial equity focus; organizing congregations and communities to engage in this work; and advocating for this cause at every level in government and in every aspect of our society.

Rev. Dr. Dietra Wise Baker, a lead organizer with Metropolitan Congregations United, describes this work as essential to her calling, and implores all of us to join in:

> I feel like the center of my call is to be a participant in the movement of building beloved community that God started a long time ago. God is calling all of us to participate in that. I find hope in my own ancestors, the stories I know

---

[70] Emma Specter, "How Kelly Loeffler's Own WNBA Team Helped Defeat Her," Vogue (Vogue, January 6, 2021), https://www.vogue.com/article/georgia-election-runoff-wnba.

in my family and of the larger Black community of where we've been, what people had to live through, and where we are now. We have come a mighty long way and have a long way to go, but let's stay in the struggle. Let's fight for the abundant life that God has for us.

I've also been thinking about when Dr. Manuel Pastor said, "The next thing is, once we tear down the stuff, have we really thought what it means to build something new? What will we build?" I don't know that we've spent as much time recreating, reimaging, and implementing the kind of structures and systems in the healthy way we want them to be. What if we win the dismantling of the policing system and the way that it's been formed? What will we put in its place? What would it look like? What would it feel like? Let's assume that we're going to win. We can't wait until we get there to start thinking about it.

The critical questions that Dietra raised in relation to a vision of hope after the current systems are dismantled are essential to understanding the type of world that we want to see. After the public execution of George Floyd in Minneapolis, calls for various kinds of police reform from restructuring police training requirements to abolishing the entire policing system were heard loud and clear. One call in particular that generated quite a bit of conversation and controversy was "Defund the police."[71] Defunding the police would require a significant reallocation of taxpayer money from policing and prisons and into public efforts such as education, housing, and healthcare for the common good. It is not necessarily a call to abolish policing but to redefine its purpose and practice by prioritizing other essential public goods that promote the well-being of all. However, the public narrative about defunding the police was conflated with the idea of abolishing the policing system and, as a result, was used as a lightning rod during the 2020 election seasons.[72]

---

[71] Sam Levin, "What Does 'Defund the Police' Mean? The Rallying Cry Sweeping the US – Explained," The Guardian (Guardian News and Media, June 6, 2020), https://www.theguardian.com/us-news/2020/jun/05/defunding-the-police-us-what-does-it-mean.

[72] Chris Cillizza, "Is 'Defund the Police' a Massive Political Mistake?" CNN Politics (CNN, June 8, 2020), https://www.cnn.com/2020/06/08/politics/defund-the-police-blm/index.html

The abolitionist movement has also garnered more attention since the killing of Floyd. Mariame Kaba is a prison industrial complex abolitionist and has worked for years to advocate for the dismantling of this system that disproportionally impacts Black people. One of her organizations is Project NIA which is a "grassroots organization that works to end the arrest, detention, and incarceration of children and young adults by promoting restorative and transformative justice practices."[73] For Kaba and many others, harm reduction occurs through the building of equitable and just communities, not policing, surveilling, and incarcerating its citizens. Activists like Kaba call us to envision and work for a society that truly promotes human flourishing and care for all, and that believes that is the best antidote to our current penal system.

Jake Lyonfields, the co-founder of the WE CAN organization in St. Louis, shares insights about the importance of the work for racial justice being understood as long-term work:

> I think one of the biggest changes since the uprising began is the networks. There is a robust network of people and there are a lot of leaders doing a lot of different things while using different strategies and tactics to achieve what they want. But there is this solid network now of people who have a direct interest in advancing racial justice in this region, and that has found a significant level of sustainability. It's not that it was sort of a white-hot flame and then it died out. I think it's a white-hot flame and it found enough fuel here locally to keep burning in a meaningful, substantive way.
>
> There has also been a much greater willingness to talk directly and openly about race and racism. That discourse has not always been pretty or painless, but there has been a willingness to talk about systemic racism. And there have been some successes at the systems level and one of the things that I am so proud of our community for doing is understanding that it is going to take a generation or more to realize what we want to change in St. Louis. That's why Forward through Ferguson was created. They launched

---

[73] "Project NIA," Project NIA, June 1, 2020, https://project-nia.org/mission-history.

their #2039 campaign, which will be a full twenty-five years after the murder of Mike Brown, saying that we want these calls to action in the Ferguson Commission report to be realized by a generation after his murder.[74]

There has been this collective understanding that progress will come in fits and starts and take many years. It's been a sad couple of years seeing the racism that is part of the DNA of this country manifest as a consequence of President Trump's election. However, we're still fighting the good fight, securing wins, and moving the needle forward.

Brittini Gray is a poet, writer, and activist who reflects on what it means for her to resist racial injustice in every way and engage in a long-term strategy for healing and transformation:

If I look at my own life, [I ask myself] how do I resist in every way possible? It's hard to try to live outside of the system and still thrive. And I see that as one of the biggest barriers to what movement spaces provide for society: the discomfort that comes with the responsibility of the dissent, the righteous dissent. I also think that how polarized our society is right now is also a barrier, because as many people as you've seen become awakened, there are a matching number of people who have become emboldened through the hate and the bigotry of rhetoric and policies that are being implemented. So I'll be honest in saying that those things make me pause and wonder what does it look like for us to get to a healed future?

And I think that the role of the healer, of the organizer, the activist, of the preacher is to paint that three-, four-, or five-hundred-year vision for people. Whatever we're fighting for now is not going to ... be realized materially for us in the blink of an eye. But how are we sowing the seeds for future generations that are going to come after us? To me, that's the hope. I mean, if you just look at the history of this country, we're only four hundred years in, and all of

---

[74] For more information on the #2039 campaign, see https://forward-throughferguson.org/implementation-2/.

this is a product and a result of the hate, the genocide, the exploitation that established this country. The good thing about where we are now is that we can look back at the Civil Rights Movement not with rose-colored glasses but with a realistic understanding of how many things we're still fighting today. And so for me, for us to continue to want to project twenty and fifty years out is idyllic rather than realistic. But for us to [en]vision five hundred years from now, [that] I think is the way to go, and communicating that to people in a way that you don't necessarily feel despair and say "Why am I doing this?" but thinking, No, really. How do I want five generations from me now to be able to live?

If we are going to live into a future filled with hope for racial justice and equality, we must reclaim our time and forge new pathways into this future. The time is now. We can't wait any longer.

St. Louis Protest on July 24, 2020 *(Photo by Philip Deitch)*

Do not get lost in a sea of despair. Be hopeful, be optimistic. Our struggle is not the struggle of a day, a week, a month, or a year, it is the struggle of a lifetime. Never, ever be afraid to make some noise and get in good trouble, necessary trouble.

—Congressman John Lewis

Epilogue

Six years have passed since our youngest son asked me if Michael Brown had received justice yet. He and his brother are teenagers now. One day last year, the three of us were walking home from a neighbor's house around the corner. It was dusk but there was still enough light for us to see. My youngest son said "Mom, I think I'm going to just run the rest of the way home." I froze in my tracks.

"No, son, don't run."

"Why mom? It's not that far."

We stood on the curb and had a conversation about why he couldn't run in our neighborhood, on the street where his dad and I pay a boatload of taxes. I had to explain to him that it's getting dark and someone might see him running and assume he's "up to no good and call the police."

He pointed to a few of our neighbors' houses and said, "But they know me." I told him "Yes, they know you and would never do anything to hurt you. But we can't control what other people might do, so we have to try and stay as safe as possible." We walked silently the rest of the way home.

Have you ever had to tell your twelve-year-old child not to run down his own street, or any residential street for that matter, because you were fearful that someone might call the police on him? If you have, you likely know how I felt in that moment. If you haven't because you never imagined that someone would think your little twelve-year-old boy is "up to no good" just because he is running at dusk, you've been given a glimpse into what daily life is like for many parents of Black children all across the country. When you hear us saying "Black Lives Matter," we are speaking out of our personal experience with all of the ways that our lives do not matter in the same way as white lives do. With all of the hope and promise that came with the passage of the Civil Rights Act in 1964, we find ourselves almost sixty years later in 2021 still fighting fervent attacks against our right to live, move, and have our being without the threat of violence against our bodies, minds, and spirits. After Bloody Sunday in Selma when John Lewis and others were savagely beaten while marching across the Edmond Pettis bridge for voting rights, spurring the passage of the Voting Rights Act in 1965, we now find ourselves in 2021 fighting the most racist and regressive voting legislation being passed in state legislatures around the country.

We cannot keep going down this racist laden road if we are going to live into a future filled with hope for all of God's children. The work of racial justice is long-term work because the foundation of white supremacy that was laid over four hundred years ago, and reinforced in every era, is inscribed in every system (economic, health, education, criminal justice, transportation, environmental, housing, and yes, even religious) that governs our society. Therefore, we must put up all of our antennas by bringing our entire selves into the work of seeing, hearing, tasting, feeling, and sniffing out racial injustice in the multiplicity of ways it presents itself. Racism has been passed down from generation to generation, and if we are ever going to chart a more just and equitable way forward, we have to make a concerted effort to break this devastating cycle in every way possible.

We are not the first people to take on this task. There have been scores of people before us that have done so and made important progress. But the struggle is not over. New battles of racial injustice are still emerging but we have to keep rising up to meet the challenges of our day. The well-being of future generations depend on the actions we take today. No, it's not easy. Yes, it requires that we put something on the line. However, inaction is a choice. And if we choose inaction in the face of racial injustice, then we are complicit in its continuation.

The good news is that in our decision to act, we are not alone. We have the "great cloud of witnesses" that have gone before us and resisted racial injustice in their own way and time. And as we see throughout scripture, God has quite a bit to say about justice. So let us reclaim our time, take heart with holy boldness, join in God's transforming work of justice in the world, rest when we need to, find joy along the way, and trust that our efforts will make a difference. We may never know the extent of the difference those efforts make, but we have faith that they will. Thanks be to God!

* * *

Jesus returned to Galilee in the power of the Spirit, and news about him spread through the whole countryside. He was teaching in their synagogues, and everyone praised him. He went to Nazareth, where he had been brought up, and on the Sabbath day he went into the synagogue, as was his custom. He stood up to read, and the scroll of the prophet Isaiah was handed to him. Unrolling it, he found the place where it is written:

> *"The Spirit of the Lord is on me,*
> *because he has anointed me*
> *to proclaim good news to the poor.*
> *He has sent me to proclaim freedom for the prisoners*
> *and recovery of sight for the blind,*
> *to set the oppressed free,*
> *to proclaim the year of the Lord's favor."*

Then he rolled up the scroll, gave it back to the attendant, and sat down. The eyes of everyone in the synagogue were fastened on him. He began by saying to them, "Today this scripture is fulfilled in your hearing." —Luke 4:14–21

Praise for Leah Gunning Francis and
Ferguson & Faith

"This is not your granny's revolution. A fresh, new, holy uprising is happening if we will only have eyes to see and ears to hear — and the courage to join them in the streets."

—Shane Claiborne, author, activist, speaker

"... an informal handbook for clergy who want to take action, and a powerful antidote to mainstream media stories and images that continue to ignore the commitment, intelligence, strategy, and integrity of the young people organizing for long-denied justice."

—Julie Polter, *Sojourners*

"Leah Gunning Francis ... brings passion to this compelling volume of stories gathered from clergy and young activists on the street in the aftermath of Michael Brown's murder. The stories will break your heart, inspire you, and motivate you to become involved in the burgeoning new civil rights movement."

—Sharon G. Thornton, *The Christian Century*

"... a powerful collection of stories of clergy and young activists who were visible and vocal in the struggle for racial justice in Ferguson. They embodied the best of the human spirit that resonated with many around the globe, and challenged this nation to live up to its ideal of liberty and justice for all."

—Emanuel Cleaver, U.S. Representative (Missouri)

9780827211056, $19.99

The Ferguson protests represented a long-smoldering movement for justice. Seminary professor, Leah Gunning Francis was among the activists, and her interviews with more than two dozen faith leaders and with the new movement's organizers take us behind the scenes of the continuing protests.

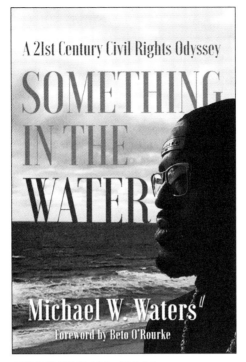

A 21st Century Civil Rights Odyssey

SOMETHING IN THE WATER

Michael W. Waters

Foreword by Beto O'Rourke

9780827235496, $16.99

"Waters, an African American pastor and civil rights activist, delivers a blistering critique of white supremacy and racial injustice in this trenchant collection of sermons, poems, and commentaries. This concise, incisive work should be a wake-up call to Americans in general and the church in particular."

—*Publishers Weekly*

9780827200999, $17.99

"*Anxious To Talk About It* is challenging, encouraging, and always faithful. Helsel's insight and wisdom strengthens our discipleship and helps us confront the impact of racism through gratitude, gift appreciation, diversity, and self-control. This book is a must-read for anyone desiring to live a spiritual life of self-discovery in the 21st century."

—Jimmie Hawkins, Director of the Presbyterian Church (USA) Office of Public Witness & United Nations

You Want to Change the World. So Do We.

Order at ChalicePress.com
or wherever you buy books.

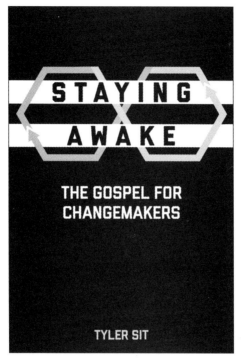

STAYING AWAKE

THE GOSPEL FOR CHANGEMAKERS

TYLER SIT

9780827235526, $16.99

"An eloquent debut...Sit's work sizzles with energy, humor, and empathy. This impressive guide conveys urgent, timely guidance for pastors, Christians, and seekers looking to marry faith and social justice."

—*Publishers Weekly*
  (STARRED REVIEW)